*The Myth*
*of the*
*Judeo-Christian*
*Tradition*

# The Myth
## of the
# Judeo-Christian
# Tradition

And Other Dissenting Essays

ARTHUR A. COHEN

SCHOCKEN BOOKS · NEW YORK

# Contents

*For my father and mother*

# Preface to the Paperback Edition

IT CAME AS no surprise to me that the original publication of *The Myth of the Judeo-Christian Tradition* was scarcely noticed by the Jewish community (excepting the astonishing and lengthy reviews of Jacob Neusner in *Midstream* and Frederick Plotkin in *Congress Bi-Weekly*), virtually ignored by Protestant thinkers, and discussed with vigor and imagination by Catholics alone. This is, in part, justified since the principal recipient of my dissent was historical Catholic theology.

What impresses me about the Catholic commentators (notably George Pepper in *The Catholic World*, Walter Arnold in *Commonweal*, and Leonard F. X. Mayhew in *The Catholic Reporter*) is their revealing insistence that my argument is too narrow, too strait-jacketed by historical presuppositions, too unyielding and obdurate before the signs of change in the Catholic world. This criticism has troubled me profoundly. If it is true, it follows that the constricted logic of my position of "Jewish-Christian enmity" must be reformulated. As the reader will see in the essays that follow, it is my contention that less than a tradition of continuity between Jews and Christians—that is, a tradition which involves the sharing of common concern and enterprise—there is at best a *traditio* of enmity and suspicion. The only common reality is that Jews and Christians divide before the same Lord, but all else, all the consequence of that division has been anger and bitterness and for the historical Jewish community considerable suffering and loss.

The new theology of Christians, the theology which was gathering strength before Vatican II in the works of Rahner, Kung, Daniélou, De Lubac and others is now, after Vatican II, the theology of an old Church become young. One has the feeling that the Catholic Church is presently two churches, a Church of the senescent (led no doubt by precisely those bishops over eighty years of age whom Pope Paul has recently excluded from voting upon his successor) and a young Church which, as though these were apostolic times once more, is seeking to reformulate the realistic bases of Christian life.

It comes forcefully to mind that Christian thinkers write today in two modes of address, the apostolic and the apocalyptic. It is true that the early Church was both apostolic and apocalyptic. It was a Church for "the between-times," after the resurrection and before the parousia, and the task of the early, unformed Church, characterized as it was by hostility and persecution from without and inchoacy within, was to maintain and extend the community of believers-in-hope. Ours are parallel times. The Church is once more beleaguered, but the primary source of its beleaguerment is not without, but within. The "persecutors" of the Church are no longer unconverted pagans, but converted pagans, or, worse, Christians relapsed into paganism (the Communist world), and even more powerfully than these political opponents, masses of believing Christians who cannot reconcile the exigencies of the world with the historical stringencies of the Church. The Church is characterized by a longing to be relevant, for relevance, however understood, is the care for efficient meaning, meaning that informs, elaborates, textures, and authenticates the life of the faithful. This concern of contemporary Christianity is deeply moving.

The religious thinking of the Jewish people is not identically animated. The Jewish people is a unity without unanimity. It is a numerical collective, inspirited by presumptions of historical continuity of belief and feeling, but without a single spirit, and hence without unanimity. Its one unanimity is its paranoid sensibility which continues to devise the world as an inhospitable place (not without reason, but also not with sufficient reason). A generation is too short to recover from the holocaust. It cannot be imagined that any thoughtful Jew, attending to the fortuity of survival and the efficiency of mass murder, can regard the world without distrust and suspicion. This is by way of clarifying the psychological valent of my insistence upon dealing with the realities of Jewish-Christian enmity. There is no Nietzschean pleasure in the affirmation of enmity, no investment in the strong, the courageous, the heroic posture of braving the hatred of the world. Such romanticism is nonsense. The critical issue is that enmity, as I have described it, is theological in form, but natural in origin. The enmity is historical. Jews and Christians have, because of fundamental differences in belief, regarded each other as objects of suspicion and worse. The forms in which such enmity has been enclosed and transmitted have been theological, from the narratives of the New Testament, through the patristic literature, Papal and Conciliar declarations, instructional and catechetical material. This literature is still employed, tacitly endorsed or glossed by some, criticized and debunked by others. It will always be this way.

In the course of time enmity may well be commingled with genuine friendship, suspicion with trust, hostility with confraternity. The moulting of time will hopefully transform Judeo-Christian enmity into Judeo-Christian humanism. It will be no less true then as now that a Judeo-Christian tradition will not have come into existence, except perhaps as an objective overview, envisaged from the outside by strangers who see fit for convenience of description to make of such profound and meaningful apposition a single continuity. But such language of tradition will continue for believing Christians and believing Jews, however much they may have come together to do the work of conserving nature and advancing the good causes of men, to be artificial and unimportant. I would much rather Jews and Christians achieve a unanimity, than a unity.

*January 1971*

# *Preface*

THE INTENTION of the essays which make up this volume is not only to break through the crust of harmony and concord which exists between Judaism and Christianity, between Jewdom and Christendom, but more to destroy that in both communities which depends upon the other for its authentication.

I thought at one time that the myth of the Judeo-Christian tradition consisted solely in the fact that Christianity was dependent in condescension upon the perduration of Israel, that the myth existed essentially for Christians, that Jews endured the myth, as they endure Christianity, as a boil which was impenetrable to the lance and would not dry up and blow away. Christianity was, in such a view, an unavoidable fact. I have now come to believe something else: the essential unbelief of both Christians and Jews. The myth, then, is more grotesque than it appears at first sight—it is the myth of Jews and Christians in *this* world (in *this* world which neither can endure) joining together to deal with the world in a newer and more grotesque *ressentiment*, a *ressentiment* based upon a dishonest compact of love and admiration. How can this be tolerated, when both conduct themselves as if God, although not yet dead, is no longer believable, and if not believable, then like some totem or scarecrow whose reality is manipulated to the cut of our notions, is become a mere construct or positing who is neither heard nor whose sounds are noticed.

The essays which form this book were written over nearly two decades. They reflect an internal consistency as well as a continuous development. The earliest essays were somewhat more polemical since, in the early 1950's, I was concerned to define my own views in distinction from those of Christian thought and, therefore, tended to use Christian doctrine as a counterfoil to my own. This tends inevitably to risk hypostatizing positions in order to facilitate distinction and self-clarification. The more abrasive examples of this I have winnowed from these texts. But what strikes me is that interpretive premises have been sustained from the earliest expressions of my views on the so-called Judeo-Christian tradition to those most recent. I have always disbelieved the premises of liberal Jewish and liberal Christian interpreters of their common ground. Common ground there is, most assuredly, but it is a ground for natural fraternity which could as easily be extruded from *de facto* social and political coexistence as from any doctrinal accommodation. In other words, it is my view that the Judeo-Christian tradition is a historicist myth.

The opening essay, "The Myth of the Judeo-Christian Tradition," and the concluding essay of this volume are the most recent. They are more than a summation. They reflect my quintessential pessimism and my quintessential optimism.

October 1, 1969

# Introduction:

## The Myth of
## the Judeo-Christian Tradition

THE JUDEO-CHRISTIAN tradition is a myth. It is, moreover, not only a myth of history (that is, an assumption founded upon the self-deceiving of man) but an eschatological myth which bears within it an optimism, a hope which transcends and obliterates the historicism of the myth. As myth it is therefore both negative and positive, deathly and dangerous, visionary and prophetic at one and the same time.

It is my intention in this discussion, first, to set forth the theological foundations upon which the myth is based and to illustrate the forms in which it has been unfolded in Western thought; second, to establish the senses in which the conception of a Judeo-Christian tradition is mythological or, rather, not precisely mythological but ideological and hence, as in all ideologies, shot through with falsification, distortion, and untruth. And, finally, since we live in postreligious times (which for the religious is an augury of the apocalypse), I hope to suggest the order of discourse which is appropriate to Jews and Christians of our day.

How can it be that Christianity, regarding itself the successor and completion of Judaism, should have elected to take into itself the body and substance of that Jewish teaching which it believed to be defective, which it regarded as having in measure rejected, in measure transformed, in measure repaired and fulfilled? How can it be that Judaism, the precedent in principle, and progenitor in history, of Christianity, should have remained not only independent but unassimilated by the doctrinal vision and historical pressure of Christianity?

This is a conundrum, but it is not without solution. Orders of existence can remain contiguous without coalescence, parallel without overlapping, related without the one disappearing into the other. But such description is not quite accurate, for such terms as continuity, coalescence, and relation describe the disposition of objects in space, whereas the essential character of the Jewish and Christian connection is a relation in time, and not in time alone but in filled time, time in which events are numbered. History is the medium in which Judaism and Christianity are sustained. There is, therefore, in addition to space *and* time, the *nexus* of events, priority and succession, formation and influence, human passion and persuasion.

Jewish and Christian time is impassioned time, time in which destinies are elaborated and consummated. Such time is the time of salvation. Jews and Christians in the first century, Jewish Jews and Jewish Christians, Jewish Jews and Gentile Christians, related less to one another as persons than to one another as bearers of the Word, as legatees and transmitters of saving truth. They could not but regard their simple flesh and their uncomplicated spirits as vessels of the Holy Spirit, the instrumentalities through whom God worked out extraordinary designs and expectations. Theirs was a personalism, but it bore less resemblance to the existential personalism with which we are today so familiar than it did to the historical realism of the Bible for which persons were immanent expressions of the divine-human tension. Biblical anthropology discloses more about God than it does about man. Biblical man, confronting himself, addressed God. He worked by a devious deduction, believing himself to be an extrusion and exemplification of the divine intention, and hence valuing his own action both inordinately and inadequately, for it was both the bearer of the ultimate intention of creation as well as a hopelessly frail, limited, inconsequential thing. One has only to regard the numerous Psalms in which man is ranked little lower than the angels and in the same breath derided and derogated. Man was person and paradox, *person* because God had made each man unique and irreplaceable, and *paradox* because every man was in himself the crossroads and meeting ground of the failure and dis-tortion of creation.

I say all this to suggest that the Jewish and Christian relation was in ancient times much too serious an engagement to become, as it has become in our time, an assumed tradition. The ancient world expected a redeemer; the Jews expected a redeemer to come out of Zion; Christianity affirmed that a redeemer had come out of Zion, but that he had come not alone for Israel but for all mankind. Judaism denied that claim, rejecting the person of that redeemer, calling his claim presumption and superarrogation, denying his mission to them (and indeed, as the Synoptic Gospels make abundantly clear, Jesus of Nazareth regarded his mission as being first and foremost, if not exclusively, to the Children of Israel, though as theologians have come to teach us Jesus did not understand either his own or God's will as well as St. Paul understood both). That same redeemer, unheard by most of Israel, rejected by its Jerusalemite establishment, was tried as an insurrectionist and brutally slain.

It matters, therefore, not at all in my view that much of Jewish and Christian doctrine is confluent, for in what does such

confluence consist; that Jews and Christians affirm an uncondi-
tional, universal, and unique God, single and undifferentiated;
that that God is believed to have created man, set man in the
midst of an ordered nature, appointed man to a destiny of service
and trust, brought near a single people—selected arbitrarily, but
nevertheless unambiguously, to be his own and through them to
bring his teaching to all the earth. These affirmations respecting
the creation, the covenant of God with his elected people-servant,
the revelation of his teaching, and the promise of redemption,
these truths, schematic, loose, general, archetypal, connect the
vision of Judaism and Christianity. But this connection is a philosophic formulation of what in the order of faith pulsates with
irrationality, passion, intensity, sharp disagreement, fissure, and
the abyss of historical enmity. I suggest in part, therefore, that
the Judeo-Christian tradition is a construct, an artificial gloss of
reason over the swarm of fideist passion. But this is not enough.
What is omitted is the philosophic (or is it a theological?) construct. What is omitted is the sinew and bone of actuality, for
where Jews and Christians divide, divide irreparably, divide finally
(though undoubtedly in the condition of finitude neither has
truth except in the adequacy of faith) is that for Jews the Messiah is to come and for Christians he has already come. That is
irreparable. It is true that Jews have made concession to the faith
of Christians, acknowledging alternately with charity or animus,
that Christians and Muslims are closer to the purity of the God-
head than are believers of the East, but this is only to reaffirm
that ultimately Israel will, employing the artifacts of Christianity
and Islam, bring all of mankind to the divine teaching of Sinai.
It is equally true that intertestamental theology and the early
Church Fathers recognized the force of Israel's refusal of Jesus
as the Christ by developing the doctrine of the Second Coming,
recognizing as they did that the end of days had not come to pass

as promised, the transformation of time and history anticipated in the immediate aftermath of the crucifixion had transpired only in the eyes of faith, and that for the public, unconverted eye there could only be the promise and persuasion of the time yet to come when Jesus would return in glory, to consummate Israel, to reintegrate Israel and the Church.

But in the meantime, between the times, between the promise of the Synagogue and the promise of the Church, what of those times? For those times (and nearly two thousand years of those times have passed), for those times what would ensue? The pavanne of death, where faith throttled faith, believer tormented believer, and the impotence of man before the magnitude of his believing overwhelmed mercy and love. We can learn much from the history of Jewish-Christian relations, but the one thing we cannot make of it is a discourse of community, fellowship, and understanding. How, then, do we make of it a tradition?

It is curious to observe that the times in which it may well have been proper to speak of tradition, men did not speak of tradition. They recognized an order of receipt and transmission, a body of sacred and secular learning which defined the substance of divine revelation and humane instruction, but they did not regard the tradition as something outside of them, as an external datum, ordered, preserved, objectified. Tradition was interior and hence did not require the sanctification and obeisance which we pay to tradition. Tradition, *traditio*, the carrying over and forward of something which was supported and sustained, was an action. It was not a passive retort to an objective datum. It was only when *traditio* was used in the sense of *receptus* or *redactio*, as something defined, ordered, or enacted that it was understood in the sense in which we now use the term. The datum received or redacted, the Word of God, finished, closed, sealed into Scripture and hence terminated as a document, describes, not the end of tradition, but the beginning of tradition. Jewish tradition is not the Jewish Bible. Jewish tradition first begins with the closing and redaction of the Bible. Until the redaction of the Bible, a Biblical tradition which kept alive the hot coal of God's Word, passing it carefully, circumspectly, but intently and with seriousness from generation to generation, reviving and reawakening it, quickening and intensifying its power, such a tradition lived. And when that tradition ran the risk of splintering, breaking, fragmenting, it was set down, redacted, confirmed, sealed, and the tradition ended—only to begin again as Rabbinic tradition which in turn was accumulated, transmitted, carried forward, developed, argued, in a word, lived, until it too became so vast, so sprawling, so subtle that it demanded redaction. The requirement of man to remember his achievements, to behold his works so that they might congratulate him is the impulse to redact the living, spoken transmission of the word into its written, dogmatic, authoritative form. Tradition is *living* when there is genuine tradition, the spoken word and the heard word surpassing the written word. It is the need to supply the spoken word with an adulterate preservative that compels us to preserve by writing. The most pristine traditions are bardic, epic, poetic, and never written. This is really only to say, as the Rabbis recognized, that in the Pentateuch God spoke and the people heard, whereas in the Prophets and writings God spoke, no longer directly, but through the medium of his saints and prophets; and in the post-Biblical literature God no longer spoke, but what was heard was an echo of his speech. This insight reverberates in the tale told by a Hasidic master who described the generational difference between himself and his teachers by explaining that when the Baal Shem Tob, the founder of Hasidism had been alive, he would go each day to a certain place in the forest, light there a fire, and say his prayers; his successor knew the place in the forest and remembered to light the fire, but no longer remembered the Baal Shem's prayer; and *his* successor no longer knew the place and could no longer light the fire; and he, in his generation, all that he could do was to tell the story. The point is, perhaps, that in our time we no longer even have the enthusiasm to tell the story, believing perhaps that even the story has become meaningless.

It is this sense of intrinsic meaninglessness which is quite possibly a significant aspect of what has come to be regarded as the Judeo-Christian tradition. Despite the intensity and seriousness with which Jews and Christians engaged in murderous polemics from the first century until the late nineteenth century (and even today the thesis has been argued by the French historian, Jules Isaac, in his book, *The Teaching of Contempt*, that Nazi anti-Semitism is a secular radicalization of the anti-Jewish impulses of historic Christianity), the polemic was characterized by the following: (1) the common conviction that the manner in which a man composed his relationship to God was central and primary to his existence; that this relationship was constitutive, and, therefore, ontological in character, and, finally, that it was a relationship which could only be regarded with absolute, albeit often dreary, seriousness; (2) the conviction that society and culture, being expressions of the relationship between man and God, could only endure and could only express their fidelity to God if they were religiously homogeneous, unmarked by dissent, disagreement, divisiveness—hence it followed that any community within the larger society which denied the prevailing and enforced homogeneity of doctrine upon which its very life was believed to depend should be either forcibly converted, driven out, or slain; (3) and lastly, between Jews and Christians an order of ignorance which, even with the modest exceptions of German and Italian humanists, remained complete and impenetrable until the age of the Enlightenment. Jews regarded Christians as at best second-best and at worst as execrable idolaters, and Christians regarded Jews as at best worthy of conversion and at worst as deicides and antichrists.

Theological fratricide, however, cannot simply be deplored. It is easy to deplore it; it is presently the easiest thing in the world of religion *to* deplore. The endless parade of Jewish thinkers addressing Christian audiences and rehearsing with calm and fluency the corruption of Christendom and the equally sincere and passionate late-flowering recognition of Christian thinkers of the enormities which Christianity has inflicted upon the Jews makes for a kind of rhapsodic, communal suffering which is finally purgative, but not really illuminating. At the same time that I would recommend that we be done with the enumeration of massacres and the exhibition of Jewish scars, I would also suggest that we can learn something by reflecting on the order of seriousness, unanimity, and ignorance upon which this historical fratricide depended.

What we can learn is how the idea of the "Judeo-Christian tradition" began and why it has become in our day a myth which buries under the fine silt of rhetoric the authentic, meaningful, and irrevocable distinction which exists between Jewish belief and Christian belief.

As I have already indicated, the notion of a Judeo-Christian tradition did not come into existence during that period which enclosed the seventeen hundred years of the origin, expansion, consolidation, and withering of Christian power. As long as Christianity could keep the enemy without the gate, it was able to maintain a species of homogeneity and community which was for all intents and purposes unassailable. In that period Christianity engaged Judaism in debate, less as a testimony to the openness of communication than as a theatrical exhibition of its power. There was no discourse, for none was felt to be needed. The argument had long since been decided by God and confirmed by the witness of the Church Triumphant.

The break in this pattern of no-communication and anti-dialogue and the transition from a closed and homogeneous society to an open and fragmented society may be traced to the extraordinary revulsion through which European society passed during the century-long wars of religion. The wars killed in the millions, but killed, it was recognized, not for the sake of the Kingdom of God, but that principalities and potentates might retain inherited power and continue to exercise it. People had ceased to be persons, as Biblical humanism would have insisted, but had become disposable units in a hieratic society in which nobility, clergy, and king stood upon mountains of corpses in order that they might reach closer to God. It was an insane time—a time, not a little like our own, in which millenarianism, the sense of doom and apocalypse, eschatological expectation flourished. But out of that massive occlusion of wasted life, there came a revulsion on behalf of man which survives to our time. If the community of the religious, as an analogue of society, could yield such desperate and hopeless folly, then religion is the enemy of man, and God and his faithful are an enormous delusion and reservoir of unreason. The effort of the *philosophes* was to both debunk the irrationality of religion and to construct a civil society grounded upon the neutralization of religion in the public domain.

Whether it is the movement from Fontenelle to Voltaire and Condorcet derisively and with authentic high humor making the religious sensibility a congerie of the fantastic, the irrational, and the antihuman or the more balanced German enlighteners, Lessing, Moses Mendelssohn, Kant, and Herder, trying to construct a social polity in which religions would be stolidly respectable, but unaggrandizing, what emerged was that European intellectuals came to regard Judaism and Christianity as essentially similar—similar not with respect to truth, but rather with respect to the untruth which they shared. Voltaire played no favorites, nor did any of the French philosophers of the Enlightenment. Christianity was the palpable enemy of reason, but Christianity grew from the delusions of Judaism, and hence Judaism was equally a ragbag of legends, superstitions, and falsities. The Judeo-Christian connection was formed by the opponents of Judaism and Christianity, by the opponents of a system of unreason which had nearly destroyed Western Europe.

It was only in the late nineteenth century in Germany that the Judeo-Christian tradition, as such, was first defined. It was introduced by German Protestant scholarship to account for the findings developed by the Higher Criticism of the Old Testament and achieved considerable currency as a polemical term in that period. There, quite clearly, the negative significance of the expression became primary. The emphasis fell not to the communality of the word "tradition" but to the accented stress of the hyphen. The Jewish was latinized and abbreviated into "Judeo" to indicate a dimension, albeit a pivotal dimension, of the explicit Christian experience. It was rather more a coming to terms on the part of Christian scholarship with the Jewish factor in Christian civilization. It was no less, for all its efforts to be scholarly, an exhibition of what Solomon Schechter called "Higher Anti-Semitism," for the Jewish in the Jewish experience was all but obliterated, being retained, rather like a prehensile tail, in the larger, more sophisticated, economy of Christian truth.

It is in our time that the "Judeo-Christian tradition" has come to full expression. It is, moreover, in our time that its mythic reality can be scrutinized. It need not be observed that the concept of the Judeo-Christian tradition has particular currency and significance in the United States. It is not a commonplace in

Europe as it is here; rather Europeans are more habituated to speak of Jewish-Christian amity, to define the foundations and frontiers of community, to describe and in describing to put to rest historic canards and libels than they are to proclaim a tradition in which distinctions are fudged, diversities reconciled, differences overwhelmed by sloppy and sentimental approaches to falling in love after centuries of misunderstanding and estrangement. Let us not speak of American secularism. So much has been written about the religion of American secularism that I would not add more (having already added enough) to this now-conventional recognition. Enough to say that there is a secular and uncritical Jacobinism abroad in the land which is neither fish nor fowl, and certainly neither Christian nor Jewish. Such secular religiosity is dangerous; it is the common quicksand of Jews and Christians. And it is here that we can identify the myth. Jews and Christians have conspired together to promote a tradition of common experience and common belief, whereas in fact they have joined together to reinforce themselves in the face of a common disaster. It is the experience not of drowning men who clutch each other as they drown, but rather of inundated institutions making common cause before a world that regards them as hopelessly irrelevant, and meaningless. The myth is a projection of the will to endure of both Jews and Christians, an identification of common enemies, an abandonment of millennial antagonisms in the face of threats which do not discriminate between Judaism and Christianity; and these threats, the whole of the Triple Revolution—automation, the population explosion, nuclear warfare—these are the threats which evoke the formation of the myth. The threats are real and desperate, but patching-over cannot suffice. The patching-over can only deteriorate further what it seeks to protect.

There can be no free Jewish reality as long as it is obliged in dialectical relation and tension with Christian history. This is not to say with Zionist ideologues that Jewish reality is always marginal reality in so far as it remains bound to the physical Diaspora and the spiritual Exile from the Promised Land. It is to say something more. For more than three centuries now Jewish reality—that is, the substance of Jewish existence, the propriety of its existence, its condition—has been contingent upon the eminence of Christian history. This is manifest not alone in the regal suffering of the Jew but in something more, for we commit ourselves to Law at a time when the very foundation of regulative Law is crumbling; we commit ourselves to the permanence of an artificial group when we no longer believe in the grounds of our own existence. Alone we have Christianity to thank for our survival. The Judeo-Christian tradition is an eschatological myth for the Christian who no longer can deal with actual history and a historical myth for Jews who can no longer deal with the radical negations of eschatology. The Christian comes to depend upon the Jew who says salvation has not yet come, to interpret for him what happens when power collapses, how men shall behave when the relative and conditional institutions of society crumble, for the Jew is an expert in unfulfilled time, whereas the Christian is an adept believer for redeemed times *only*. The Christian comes to depend upon the Jew for an explanation of unredeemedness. The Jew, on the other hand, must look to Christianity to ransom for him his faith in the Messiah, to renew for him his expectation of the nameless Christ. This is the center of the Jewish-Christian nexus, but such a nexus has just begun in our times. It is not yet a tradition, for it has just been born out of the crisis which threatens all humanity. However, if it continues to be supported as a myth, if it becomes as myths become when they have lost their contact with the living sources of truth in human life, mere devices of masking the abyss, then we shall, as Jews and Christians, perish.

Ours is a time not of institutions and dominions and centers of power. If we surrender to these we are surely lost. This is a time—and the time of the apocalypse is always such a time—when men must speak *out* of their differences and *over* the chasm that separates them. It is not that Christians should suspend their faith that they may learn to speak well and learnedly with Jews or that Jews should inhibit their eccentric singularity that they may learn to identify the better with Christians. It is that Christians must learn to speak through Jesus Christ to that in the world which is untransformed and unredeemed and Jews must learn to speak out of Torah with a sagacity and mercy which brings the world closer to its proper perfection. There is a new communication—not of artificial traditions and hypothesized concords, but a communication of friendship in the holy spirit which is an order of love that is born out of faith in the urgency of the quest, rather than in the certitude of the discovery.

*The Myth*
*of the*
*Judeo-Christian*
*Tradition*

# I. Foundations and Definitions, Theological and Historical

# The Past and Future of
# Eschatological Thinking

## Characteristics of Eschatological Thinking

ESCHATOLOGY is the doctrine of "the last things." It interprets that moment at which the phenomenal world—the world of time and space, nature and history—comes to an end. Violently construed, the *eschaton*, the ultimate moment, marks the destruction of terrestrial history and the advent of the reign of God.

At the same time, however, that we make mention of "last things," we should hasten to add that this rendering of the Greek term *eschatos* is already a definition which limits and interprets as it defines, for to speak of "last things"—however vague and imprecise and uncompromising this may seem—is already a *view* of eschatology. Implicit to our understanding of "last things" is a concentrated focus upon the end of the commonplace world with which our life is ordinarily preoccupied; moreover, this focus ignores the crucial fact in our Western understanding of eschatology that these last things are not last in the sense of being end-moments in a linear historical progression, but last because, through an action external to it (a juncture of the terrestrial and the extraterrestrial), an end-event occurs. It is more proper, therefore, to speak of eschatology as the doctrine of "the last event," for the word *event* suggests an action, not simply a state of being

3

—an action, moreover, which is prefigured and anticipated throughout the course of history and has, therefore, special meaning for those who have awaited it.

What, then, are the characteristics of the eschatological event? (1) It is either one single event radically juxtaposed and unrelated to all previous historical events, or a culminating event, prefigured and formed by all previous historical events; (2) it is an event which occurs within the order of time and space, or else is an ultimate event which crystallizes at the same time that it annihilates time and space; (3) it is a "relational" event internally connected with and implied by everything historical; (4) it is an event which is "meaningful," for it interprets history for the historian (and here we consider every man to be a historian in so far as he reflects upon historical events with a view to self-understanding), or it is an event which, in more radical eschatological doctrine, explicates the meaning of all history, suggests that toward which history has been directed and for which purposes it has been intended; (5) and, last, whether the eschatological event occurs many times or is, as classic eschatologists thought, a single and irrevocable event, it is nevertheless a symbolic event which points *really* to that which transcends history and is its ground. It is symbolic for the simple reason that if it occurs many times, it becomes eschatological only for the believer who seeks within it the prefigurings of the consummation for which faith longs and if it is a single, cataclysmic event there is no judge who survives to estimate whether expectation and occurrence conform— whether such images as the reign of God, the judgment of history, the transfiguration of the saved, the resurrection of the dead indeed occur. Eschatology is thus mythological doctrine which undoubtedly beclouds and conceals a true symbolic assertion regarding man's locus in history, God's relation to history, and the community of man and God in the transformation of history.

These are the elements of eschatological doctrine—a view of man, the immersion of man in historical time and natural space, the seeking of man to locate himself beyond the flux and relativities of time and the static positioning of space, the conviction that as God confirms man's faith, He also authenticates the entelechy and goal of history. Eschatology is that doctrine, therefore, which unites man's trust in God with man's equally considerable passion to invest history with meaning. Narrowly conceived, there has been only one great age of eschatological thinking—the period of late Jewish prophetic and apocalyptic thought (from Deutero-Isaiah through the Book of Daniel and immediately thereafter) and early Christian apocalypticism reflected in the Gospels and the Pauline literature. Although subsequent revivals of eschatological thinking were to recur with man's reflections on historical disasters past and to come (St. Augustine, Martin Luther, and to a lesser extent numerous secular and theological thinkers in our own day), undiluted and spontaneous eschatology is a phenomenon of the Hebrew Bible, the Gospels and the Epistles. All eschatological thinking, which follows this earliest and pristine period, is characterized by an effort to come to terms with the predicaments created by the image of man and history which it had projected, and the failure of God to confirm its expectation. All postscriptural eschatology is limited to a commentary upon the failure of scriptural eschatology. This is a critical weakness of eschatological thinking which would seem to make all modern efforts at its renewal unavoidably barren and unproductive, for if the conditions of discourse are limited to a fixed and final historical event which is long since past, eschatological thinking is perforce restricted to the commentary and interpretation of a single, penultimate historical event. Eschatological thinking cannot, under such limitations, arise out of the present moment to confront the future with fresh insight unless the Bible is understood less as a finality than as an open and figural adumbration of the future.[1]

The unfortunate penalty which is paid for limiting historical eschatology to the short period which compasses the late books of the Hebrew Bible and the New Testament is that eschatology is essentially a special (however radical and specific) example of the metaphysics of history. As long as there is an effort to interpret the character and causality of history, there is an equally profound effort to define its meaning and purpose. The metaphysics of history (less a metaphysics of the historical event than a metaphysics of man, the creature who is preeminently historical) is prior to the emergence of eschatology, for the understanding of man's historicity precedes both in time and being the specific constructions of eschatology. The books of the Bible which announce and develop the providential course and development of the people of Israel take the historicity of man for granted. The convocation of the Hebrew people carries with it, beside all other commandments, the implicit and assumed "commandment" that the Hebrew understand himself as a creature of history—always liable to the temptations and possibilities of the historical moment, always open to the corrosive influence of the alien and the demanding corrective of God, always sensitized to the manner in which nature and history are interwoven by God to reward and chastise his activity. Hebrew thinking until the Babylonian exile was historical, although not eschatological. It always interpreted history—seeking out its origin and consequence—although its un-

1. This has the effect, if accomplished, of changing one's approach to the Bible from that of either a literal fideism or formal rationalism into the kind of approach which Bultmann, in one way, describes as the attitude of hermeneutics or which I have described as the way of "existential dogma." Cf. *The Natural and the Supernatural Jew: An Historical and Theological Introduction*, Pantheon, New York, 1962, Introduction.

derstanding of Providence was rooted in the finitude of life and the exigencies of its natural and political environment. The Hebrew view of history which prepared for and shaped the eschatology which would arise out of catastrophe was oriented to immanent fulfillment within history. But such was a metaphysics of history. However implicit and unexpressed, the Hebrew understanding of man was formed by categories which defined and interpreted the historicity of man. The Hebrew metaphysics of history raised questions which would later become central to eschatology, for it wondered about the goal and destiny of its historical life. It matters little whether its understanding of history was as precisely formed by eschatological concerns as was the Apocalypse of Daniel or St. Paul's letter to the Romans; what matters is that any effort to define the meaning and goal of history (however much that meaning and goal may be understood to be rooted in the immanent movement of events) gives reality and significance to eschatological interpretations.

What differentiates eschatology from the philosophy of history (distinguished justifiably from the metaphysics of history), what permits it to share more in common with metaphysical speculation than with traditional rational and empirical philosophy, is that eschatology seeks not only the external form and observable causality of history but also its internal spirit. Eschatology seeks to penetrate the shapes and constellations of historical events to the inner spirit which may be called their freedom. Freedom is at the heart of history—it matters little that man is a creature bound to his historical condition, that acting man is historical man, if the source of his action is not free. However much man may be linked to nature, however much he may be a highly sophisticated product of nature, when he acts he transcends his connection to nature, he exceeds his coterminal connection with his environment, he becomes historical and he becomes free.

7

## A Short History of Eschatological Thinking

Modern eschatology, such as it is, is the bearer of two traditions—the tradition of classic eschatology, which is marked and stamped with failure, and the idea of history, as it developed following the disappointment of eschatological expectation.

The sense of history, however immanent and anchored in the thought of Biblical man, was not explicit as doctrine. History as a concept is not Biblical, but history as a reality suffuses the Bible. The Biblical historical sense prepared the way for the eschatological expectations of the late Hebrew tradition and its rabbinic legatees as well as for the early Christians. The eschatological sense was a special historical sense, a crystallization and condensation of the historical sense, a sharpening and focusing of the whole of history to a single point, a transformation of the psychological temper from awareness and exposure to all history as the bearer of hope to the anticipation of a single event which would eclipse all previous history and consummate it.

The oldest tracings of the sense of history do not appear as historical thinking, but as myth. Such myths are devised and transmitted to give coherence to what is not yet coherent, to structure and organize a universe for which no instruments of interpretation are available. The Babylonian cosmogonies, much like the myths of Sudanese tribesmen, or those of the peoples of New Guinea, or the aborigines of Australia, are means of coming to terms with the essential processes of nature, the mysterious fact of existence, and the psychological necessities which provoke men to the remarkably human effort to explain the fact of their own life. Such myths bear resemblance to history because they narrate events which connect man's own origins with supernatural personalities who lived, loved, died, and were reborn in them.

It is only when a people coheres into a nation, acquiring in addition to a divine lineage a lineage of historical events, that consciousness gives birth to historical memory. In the ancient world the myths of the Greeks or the narratives of the Assyrian kings center upon memorable events, important personages, heroic deeds —the recollection of these invest the routine of days with the emphatic underscoring of the poetic imagination. It is no longer mythological history; it is history so mixed with poetry that we properly describe it as epic. Epic does not have the purpose of simply providing a record of human acts, but rather of testifying to the grandeur of human origins.

In its earliest moments mythology may be polarized and contrasted with eschatology. Where the most ancient myths of man concern his origins and beginnings, eschatological mythologies concern his end—less the terror of death than the mystery of life agitates the most primitive level of the human psyche (it is for this reason that many primitive cultures cannot really believe, as Ernst Cassirer has noted, in the reality of death). Clearly, however, there can be no history if the only speculation is upon events that signalize the origin of man or on discrete and exemplary occurrences which reassure man of the importance of his beginnings. There can be historical thinking only when man becomes aware of his own finitude and of his own death, for death is every man's *eschaton*.

## History According to Herodotus and Thucydides

Herodotus undertook to recount the history of the Greeks, as he observes, "lest the deeds of men should fade in the course of time, and the great and marvelous works which Greeks and Barbarians have performed should be without glory, and especially for what reason they carried on war against each other." The role of the historian at this early moment in Western civilization is to provide memory with the promptings and recollections of human achievement which enable it to supplement the instruction of the moralist with the evidence of history. And it could not be otherwise, for the Greek understood man to be embedded in nature, a sophistication and specialization of principles found in nature. Since man was a natural creature, his acts were to be investigated with the same degree of precision and with a view to the same degree of clarity as the investigation of any natural phenomenon. In such a view history could not be distinguished from nature, other than for the common observation that historical phenomena, being essentially transitory and subject to the caprice of memory, were less worthy objects of study. Since every practical science had as its end the education of virtue, the historical memory could be useful if it aided the formation of character. However, since history is an imprecise science, it is less serviceable even than poetry, for where poetry imitates discriminable human actions, distributing praise and blame according to merit, it is more difficult to determine the specifics of historical action and, therefore, more difficult to employ history in the instruction of man.

Since history was written in order that Herodotus might recollect the great and glorious works of man, the role of the gods was limited to their participation in the unfolding or inhibition of human purpose. The gods function in Herodotus as but glosses upon otherwise palpably human activity; they are treated as so many agents, among other agents, of human activity. To be sure, they define the ever present background of fate to which both gods and mortals were liable, but they play a less significant role in the history of Herodotus than they earlier played in Greek popular religion and mythology. However, where Herodotus will permit the gods to chasten and correct, Thucydides succumbs to no such temptation. For him the action of history is wholly analogous to that of the cosmos; change is but the same reality appearing amid a new constellation of events—each element is the same, although the arrangement and patterning of history may vary.

The historiography of Herodotus and Thucydides is turned toward the past, not toward the future. The value of history consists in learning the lessons of the past in order that the past might be glorified in the memory of the living and imitated in the character and action of men. It is not concerned with informing man's attitude toward the future. The future could have little significance for a civilization which conceived the universe to be without beginning and end, whose understanding of freedom was inhibited by fate, whose orientation was to the imitation of the perfections of nature, and which believed that the practice of virtue could ensure the happiness of the wise.

## History According to the Hebrew Bible

A different sense of history than the Greek informs the Scriptures of ancient Israel. The Bible commences with the assumption that the privileged people are, therefore, the most likely to err. Where for the Greek *hubris* is a defect of the individual, among the Hebrews the danger of excess and transgression is collectivized and ascribed to the entire people. Biblical history is recounted, therefore, not to improve the political counsels of its leaders or to sophisticate the moral judgments of its priests, but to instruct the whole nation. Even in the earlier Jahwist and Elohist histories of the Bible, history is narrated with some view of its unifying end—the integration of the nation in fulfillment of divine promise to the Patriarchs. In the later books of the Bible, the antiphon most characteristic of the Hebrew view of history becomes emphatic—divine instruction and human waywardness, divine warning and human transgression, man's disobedience and sin and God's justice and remission of sin, man's penance and God's forgiveness.

With the intrusion of the prophetic witness into the Biblical canon, the focus of error and forgiveness is as sharpened as it is broadened. No longer Israel, the single people—isolated and unconnected—but the people as a vehicle of world history comes under the dominion of God. Israel is transformed by even the most ardently nationalistic prophets into a bearer of all history. The first glimmerings of paradigmatic history, inner history (as contrasted with the external flow of events) emerges. The connection and obligation of Israel to Assyria, Babylon, and Egypt, Phoenicia, and the lands beyond the seas comes to the fore. It does not come to the center merely because Israel has had dealings with these nations, has conquered or been conquered by them; but rather because it begins to understand its place in history, not as one in which terrestrial triumph or defeat really matters, but as one in which right and wrong action shift the divine balance to the side of justice or mercy.

The ancient Hebrew believed that what he did mattered to God and what God desired mattered to history. This interconnection was an authentic novelty. History ceased to be an analogue to nature and became a unity fashioned by rubrics of action and conduct whose origin could not be construed as historical. The God of Israel, unlike the gods of paganism, did not hover over nature, inserting himself into nature to sport with or discomfit the pretensions of man; God was immanent as a person addressing persons (and as such within nature) and transcendent as author, instructor, director, and counselor to history (and, as such, beyond nature).

The Hebrew view of history is not yet eschatology, but it already pre-empts the characteristic modes of any metaphysics of history. These modes are not stated as such because the Hebrew mind abhorred abstraction; but, in its insistence upon the interconnection and unity of historical events—both horizontally as they unfold from the creation and accompany the gathering and integration of the Hebrew peoples—and vertically—as God enters history to express its potency and possibility—a metaphysical view of history has been affirmed. It is a metaphysics which cannot, however, conceive of history as a simple whole. Since the understanding of history is complicated for the Hebrew by his incommensurability with God, he can speak of the wholeness of history synoptically and synthetically, but never completely: *synoptically* in that man, in his unaided finitude, can only distill meaning from memory, and *synthetically* in that, with the revealed perspective of God, he is availed of the principles with which to clarify his apprehension of Providence.

## Eschatology Without the End: Jewish Apocalypticism

The idea of the *eschaton* enters man's reflections upon history at that moment at which he is prepared to accept the requirement of completion and perfection while acknowledging the retrogressive and sinful capacities of his nature. At such moments man shifts his focus from creation to salvation, from origin to end, from life to death. It is no wonder that for the Hebrew, death was utterly final and unmitigated as long as history was seen as a process which emerged, with creation, out of chaos. It is equally no wonder that the Hebrew view of history was dialectical, an alternation of divine demand and human response, essentially incomplete and uncompletable. The dimension of the eschatological entered Hebrew thought following the catastrophic Babylonian exile. The Babylonian exile registered two authoritative dissents from a simplistic dialectic: it affirmed that God not only could but would use *all* of history to bring his elected people to his service and, second, it introduced into the historic consciousness the awareness that history suffers from violent quakes and dislocations which anticipate and prefigure a consummate end. Henceforth, not the interlocutions of the patriarchs with God or the judges and kings of Israel with God, but the whole people and all of history would be incorporated into the schema of Providence.

Eschatology is, Rudolf Bultmann has suggested, the product of cosmic mythology historicized. It emerges as a result of man's transference of the periodicity of nature—the cycle of the seasons, the course of the heavens, the generation and destruction of natural life—to the sphere of history. If spring is born and dies amid the snow, if the sun rises and disappears, if the flower buds and decays, why is not human life, culture, society, indeed history, similarly patterned to be born and to die? The cyclical movement of time and nature, a view common to the Greek and Hellenistic world, was first rationalized in Greek science and historicized in late Jewish thinking. The Book of Daniel, for example, develops the idea of the four kingdoms to suggest the rise and degeneration of humanity. This notion of Daniel has its clear basis in Babylonian tradition according to which each era is ruled by an astral deity who is fashioned from a different metal (Daniel 2). With Daniel is born that most eschatological idea of the two kingdoms—the kingdom of history in which Israel vanquishes its enemies (the kingdom of terrestrial salvation) and the prior history of the world before the era of salvation commences, in which Israel is subject and in sufferance (the kingdom of evil). This dualism, later developed by Jewish apocalypticism, is taken up by St. Paul, defined more radically again by Marcion and the Gnostics, and restored in yet a different form by St. Augustine. The Book of Daniel is an atypical document of late Judaism; however, it does not yet bespeak the insights and categories which came to mark the eschatological sense of Christianity. Bultmann is right, therefore, in affirming that "in the Old Testament there is no eschatology in the true sense of a doctrine of the end of the world and a succeeding time of salvation." The question which one might ask is whether true eschatology need be Christian. Is the truth of eschatological doctrine its accommodation to established historical models (in which case Bultmann is surely correct) or its appropriateness to the condition of man and history?[2]

The dualism of the two kingdoms according to Daniel is radicalized by Christian thought in its uncompromised polarity of the God of salvation and the God of creation. Such a polarity is essentially alien to Judaism. The God of the Hebrew Bible does indeed judge and redeem, but it is judgment and redemption within history, not upon it. God always appears to act within the moment and never external to it. This, of course, creates enormous weakness of doctrine, for history is never conceived in Judaism to be closed or ended—as such, it is really possible to speak of history only synoptically or synthetically as I have suggested, but never completely. As long as the consummation of history is historical, there is no judgment beyond history other than the disclosures

---

2. If the latter, as I believe, it is really not possible to develop an eschatology unless one is also prepared to develop a doctrine of the interrelation of God, man, and history. Although I do not avoid this problem I have tried toward the end of this essay as well as in the closing chapter of my book, *The Natural and the Supernatural Jew*, to define some of the conditions of Jewish eschatology.

of revelation to history. This would seem to compromise Jewish messianism, indeed the Jewish doctrine of salvation; for the messiah comes to work in history, and salvation is salvation of historical time. The messianic accession is never in Jewish thought (with the exception of works such as the Book of Daniel and not even truly there) an end of history. But this weakness—and it is a weakness which leads to incredible mythologizing of both the Jewish nation and the messianic age—is compensated for by an honest and convincing realism. Judaism must always explain to itself the defeats of history, and its explanation is always crudely dependent upon the assumption of divine punishment and exculpation. It does not, however, have to explain why history goes on even though the virtual "end of history" has come. Even though the eccentric German scholar, Hans Joachim Schoeps, believes this claim of strength to be a naïve argument against Pauline theology, it is a gravely serious one: according to Jewish lights there is no caesura in history which requires that an antihistorical dogma be set into the center of ongoing historical life.[3]

It is crucial to recognize that, in the Biblical perspective, the nature and interpretation of history are inseparable from the nature and understanding of eschatology. In its beginnings the idea of history was an unconscious distillation from the mythologies of eschatology—the preprophetic and prophetic view of the cov-

---

3. "We do not perceive any caesura in history. We recognize in it no middle term, but only an end, the end of God's ways, and we believe that God does not interrupt his course. For us redemption is indissolubly one with the consummation of creation, with the establishment of the divine unity, no longer frustrated, suffering no contradiction, realized in the multiplicity of the world, one with the fulfilled sovereignty of God. We are unable to understand the idea of an anticipation of this consummation experience by one section of humanity, whose souls are already redeemed." Martin Buber, *Die Stunde und die Erkenntnis,* Schocken Verlag, Berlin, 1936, pp. 153 f.

enanted relation of man and God and the anticipation of God's righteous rule through his anointed is eschatological teaching which reveals the Hebrew doctrine of history. At this moment, centuries and philosophies later, the recovery of the eschatological sense is brought about only through a rethinking of our understanding of history. Depending upon where one stands (whether one takes history as the stage upon which the intimacies of the divine-human encounter are played out or whether one takes history as the self-contained and self-interpreting whole for which all transcending exegesis is captious, false, and mythological) one has history with eschatology or history without eschatology. But whichever way one speaks of history one asks about its purpose and meaning (which is virtually to ask an eschatological question) and if one asks about the *eschaton* one is deeply and inextricably involved in history. It follows then that any doctrine of the end which severs the ending from the process which it ends (as did those paradoxes which juxtaposed the pure to the impure eons or the formalistic views which speak of the end as an act of supernature without connection with the nature which it consummates) is false. The beginning in creation and the end in salvation must unfold through history. It is with the matter of history that God must deal, for in creation he created the drama of history and in the *eschaton* he completes that drama—between beginning and end the drama must be played.

Apocalyptic Judaism—a Judaism already heavily infiltrated by Iranian dualism and Hellenistic anxiety—expanded the idea of the two eons, the two kingdoms, and the two ages into an authentic eschatology. This apocalypticism, however, did not establish itself in the synagogue nor did it come to shape the basic emphases of the rabbinic mind other than by sharpening and accenting the alienation of apocalyptic movements from normative Judaism. According to apocalyptic eschatology—as it is found represented in IV Ezra, the Syriac Baruch, the Psalms of Solomon and such literature, the individual is spun out of the community to fend for his own salvation—and he fends well, for he is assured that when the final judgment comes he will be judged according to his own merit, that the community of the elect and sanctified will be ransomed from the fire, and that he will be among them. In such a view God no longer redeems the righteous community, raising up the individual to the perfection of his fellowship, but rather the individual in the age of apocalypse is splintered off from the community to work out his own salvation.

The ambiance of the first-century apocalyptic eschatology into which Jesus of Nazareth was born was not a single community of common mind and undivided attitude. Over and against the apocalyptists who feared death and despaired of redemption within history there were many myriads of the House of Israel who were satisfied to give pleasure to God, to do his work, and leave the Day of the Lord to his own devising. This quiet Pharisaism, long unknown and still unknown, remains an enduring counterbalance to the common impression of a first-century world full of agitation, enthusiasm, and the sense of defeat.

## EARLY CHRISTIANITY

In the New Testament, although the view of history defined by the Hebrew Bible is preserved, the apocalyptic view prevails. It is generally agreed by New Testament scholars that the reign of God which Jesus announced is the eschatological reign. The only question which remains is whether Jesus believed that the reign of God was *shortly* to arrive or rather that the advent of the *eschaton* was imminent or fulfilled in his own life, ministry, and death. There is little doubt but that Jesus believed that the attitude of others toward him was decisive—that is, that they were marked off or included in the imminent Kingdom by the position which they assumed toward him (Mark 2:18; Luke 10:18, 10:23 f.). But at the same time as Jesus saw his own generation to be "adulterous and sinful" (Mark 8:38) he affirmed that those elected by grace to believe in him would be saved. Unlike the late prophets of Israel, such as Isaiah and Deutero-Isaiah, he did not project the future of history beyond his own age to an age yet to come. His was, at least in the pristine sense of his teaching, the penultimate era which would be followed by the end, the resurrection of the dead, the salvation of his disciples, and divine judgment upon the unfaithful. The teaching of Jesus, however much it may be only a radicalization of prophetic tradition, is not to be understood—as Martin Buber has—as that of one of the suffering servants concealed in the unfathomable resource of divine instruction (to be hidden or revealed for the illumination of history), for Jesus, unlike the prophets, held out no hope to the future of man. His age, Jesus seems to affirm, was the consummating age and, if he be prophet, he is the last (and therefore truly no prophet, for there is no future to come).

In the rhythm of the narrative of the Gospels, Jesus ministers, is apprehended, tried, judged, crucified, and on the third day, according to the testimony of those who saw the empty tomb and were visited by him in posthumous revelation, he rose to glory to pass judgment upon man and the nations. It is here, upon this structure of quasihistorical recitation, that the problematic of Christian eschatology begins. For with Jesus came not the End, and after Jesus the End was still awaited, and beyond the end of waiting a new image was demanded which would justify the continuing demand of the End, while rationalizing its failure to occur.

The Christian community that was born between the death of Jesus and the elaboration of Pauline Christianity was not a continuation of the Jewish community. At the same time as Western investment in "the Judeo-Christian tradition" continues to accumulate, it should be noted that for the Jew there is not (rightly understood) such a tradition and for the Christian what is taken as Jewish is either a caricature of Judaism or a new construction of it. In neither alternative is there essential connection, although both communities survive the demands and exactions which each makes upon the other. The Christian community conceived itself for but a short time as bound by ties of lineage and genealogy to the community out of which it grew. Such ethnic connection evidently proved to be as hobbling to the new Church as it proved illusory and deceiving to the Jew. In seeing itself as a branch fashioned by God and grafted upon the stock of Israel, Paul expresses the exquisite irony and seriousness of Christianity's nexus with Judaism (Romans 11:23–24). The entire tradition of Israel is now to be read with the light that glows from the new eon, which illumines the shadowings and limnings of Christian possibility in the history of the Hebrews. The covenanted and elect community of Israel is sustained less by the cognition of its independent reality or as an eschatological countervalence than as a pious history full of allusion and animadversion to Christian promises.

Bultmann rightly describes the early Christian community as follows: *"The new people of God* has no real history, for it is the community of the end-time, an eschatological phenomenon."[4] With such a view it is no wonder that the ethical injunctions of Jesus and the moral teachings of the Gospels sustain the force of traditional Judaism, for in the between-time which separates the incarnation from the end, positive Judaism remains binding, while

4. Rudolf Bultmann, *History and Eschatology*, University Press, Edinburgh, 1957, p. 36.

only preparatory fasts and abstinences are introduced to ready the believer for the consummation. The intervening ethic of the early Christian community is unoriginal (nor need it have been, given its eschatological preoccupation). Even Christian love is directionless, for it is not formed by specific tasks and obligations —it is a pure generality. And so it must be, for one cannot love and serve and work for a creation and a history which is shortly to be overwhelmed. In short, for early Christianity eschatology consumed history.

Jesus did not return. However, Mark (13:30–37) and II Peter (3:4) move to interpret the delay, their gentle explanations fall leaden upon hearts that await the parousia in each instant. It is to this predicament of Christianity that the Pauline and Johannine answers are directed.

Since history up to the Incarnation and Crucifixion is, according to Paul, a history of sin, there can be no natural unfolding and natural correction of history. History is not self-regenerative. If it could restore itself, Paul reasons, it would have no need of incarnate grace nor could it accept and rationalize the grotesque death of its redeemer. History must end and its end must be brought about external to the processes of history. The goal of history is no longer within history but beyond it. God must end history to confirm Jesus as Christ. But this end, even though it cannot be founded upon historical events nor apprehended by a philosophy of history, is nevertheless given to history. God confers meaning upon history in the sense that he required the eon of sin that it might ache for the eon of grace. This bizarre—and to my view incomprehensible—Pauline dualism arises less from Pauline theology, strictly taken, than from Pauline anthropology. Jesus to be Christ does not necessitate the Pauline view of history, but rather the Pauline view of history necessitates Jesus as Christ. Paul's suspicion and contempt for the pretensions of man to fulfill the will of God require that man be given over to sin that he might be ransomed by the grace which he believed to be in Jesus Christ. It is out of this Pauline polarity of the kingdom of the fallen Adam (ruled by the Law and condemned to sin) and the kingdom of Christ (ruled by a most unpolitical and impolitic grace) that the precious paradoxes of Christian faith arise.

The anthropology of Paul is possible only because he is deeply sensitive to the historicity of man. Man is a creation who acts and whose action before God defines him as either free or in bondage. If he imagines that he is ever liberated from his past subjection to sin, he is without grace; it is only when he recognizes that he can never relinquish his past, that he must make his peace with it and come to each new situation in order that he might become a new being before his future—without illusion and self-deception—that he achieves freedom and grace. Man's historical life is validated by faith. Thus, for Paul, history and grace become intertwined. The Pauline solution to the delay of the parousia of Christ is based upon man's historicity, upon man's having to satisfy the demands of renewal in the historical situation.

In the between-time which separates the believer coming to believe and the parousia, what happens might be termed the routinization of eschatology (routine being understood as the renewed sense of continuous and unending historical life). History must now go on between the eschatological event past and the eschatological event anticipated. At the same time the believer must be sustained and comforted, assured and confirmed—and out of this human demand to support historical life in the between-time the sacramental system of Christianity emerges. The sacrament links the past and the future, taking both in one. But centuries elapsed and the enthusiasm which greeted Pauline expectation was institutionalized. The Church looked to its own history, became part of the world, wedded itself to the world in order to survive the world and, in the course of time, passed its eschatological enthusiasm through the wringers and dampers of historical vicissitude.

## THE NEUTRALIZATION OF ESCHATOLOGY

St. Augustine's argument in *The City of God* provides the clue to the secularization of eschatology in the Age of Enlightenment. Augustine sets the drama of salvation on the stage of history—it is not God outside and beyond history, but God amid history who effects the achievement of its ends; moreover, history is now fashioned out of the human decision and the decisive event. The struggle between the terrestrial city and the city of God could be likened to the teleological view of history constructed by the ancients to provide the groundwork for a wholly secular view of history, for the struggle of the two cities could be reinterpreted—as it was—to mean that man had lost sight of virtue, fallen into ignorance and lust, but was freed from these by the rediscovery of reason and right conduct. This view, secularizing as it does the Augustinian view, is joined with a teleology which describes the tension of history as the struggle of the irrational forces in man and nature with science and rational understanding.

In the *Scienza Nuova* of Giambattista Vico the idea of a goal and consummation of history is eliminated. In its place the thesis of *course* and *recurrence* (*corso e ricorso*) comes to define the push and movement of history replacing the activity of divine intelligence. Indeed, Vico—pious son of the Church though he was—eliminates God from history. Having fulfilled the task of inseminating history with a natural light, Vico is able to relinquish history to unfold according to a natural, rational, internal logic.

Immanuel Kant, although preserving the idea of a teleology

of history, considers its *telos* to be wholly immanent, to be the achievement of a rational and moral society within history. Pressing further along the same path, Hegel preserved the Christian understanding of history as an integral unity, but abandons any notion of Providence as being insufficiently rational. The divine plan which imparts unity to history is imposed by the Absolute Mind which passes, not through the neat cycles of Vico toward its end, but through the agonies of affirmation, denial, and synthetic reconciliation. History is a tension of events pressing toward unity and self-clarification. The goal of history is not in the remote future but in the process whereby history and absolute mind come to unity. The Christian moment in history is considered by Hegel to be absolute religion, because in Christ the unity of mind and history is prefigured.

The Hegelian metaphysical dialectic is transformed into dialectical materialism by Karl Marx. Marx retains the dialectical movement, but makes matter rather than mind its fundamental substance—matter here understood as those powers and forces in society and nature which are subject to an inexorable causation. Marx separates history from nature—a separation he could more effectively perform than could Hegel—for Marx sees the motives of historical events in the matter of socioeconomic life, not in the whole play of human forces which includes man's natural and biological life along with his social and intellectual life. All historical forms are seen by Marx as ideological masquerades which seek to perpetuate injustice and corruption. Only through their destruction by a realistic materialism could a "Kingdom of God" without God be instituted. Historical materialism completes the secularization of eschatology.

The line which runs from Vico through Marx defines a secularization of eschatology through the devices of idealism—a running of the course from idealism to its antipode in materialism.

There is, however, a countertrend of secularization which emerges from the doctrine of progress. Although, to be sure, an affirmation of progress is made by both Hegel and Marx, the notion of man's uninterrupted move toward a terrestrial utopia is more properly located in the French Enlightenment of the eighteenth century. The faith in unlimited progress originated in a polemic against the Biblical understanding of Providence. Even before Voltaire sought to deliver the West from a Christian teleology of history, Fontenelle (1657–1757) had tried in his *Origin of Fables* to demonstrate the questionable foundations upon which the fantasies of Providence were founded.[5] Indeed, the tradition of humane reason—a Stoic tradition which is renewed in Erasmus and taken up later by Montaigne, Montesquieu, Fontenelle, and other *philosophes* of the eighteenth century—had long insisted that much which religion imports into history reason might justifiably debunk. What begins as an insistence that reason be allowed to vacate the cobwebs of superstition ends with the insistence that reason replace Providence, that reason become its own lawmaker, its own providence, and finally in Comte's temples of reason, its own divinity. Voltaire, Turgot, Condorcet, and later Comte and Saint-Simon sustain a tradition in which the perfection of science and the accumulation of knowledge will enable man properly to assess his past, learn its lessons, and perfect his future. Although the idea of the unity of history is preserved, Providence is dispatched in favor of a secular version of the teleology of history, which consists in progress promoted by science. Eschatological perfection is secularized to mean the increasingly abundant comfort, security, and wisdom of mankind.

5. See Albert Salomon's discussion of Fontenelle in his book, *In Praise of Enlightenment*, Meridian Books, New York, 1963.

## THE PRESENT CONDITION OF
## ESCHATOLOGICAL THINKING

History outlives its modes of exegesis and interpretation. Reason has not brought us to perfection nor has an immanent divinity (whether it be mind or the entelechy of society) realized the unity which it presumed. Views of history in which the goal is itself part of the historical process have not proved notably fruitful; nor have eschatological doctrines proved serviceable or meaningful. We are left, as we were before, with incomplete history. And yet in this particular aberrant age it has become ever more relevant to ask, to what end is history? May man acquire from history a meaning and instruction? Does history express a formal structure, a unity, a *telos*? Does history point itself to an end-moment or does God fashion, in his own good time, an end-moment to history? This is only to ask, is eschatological thinking relevant? Are the elaborate structures which apocalyptic Judaism and Pauline Christianity sharpened meaningful? Or are they but chimeric constructions which men project to allay despair, to transform and purge death of its finality, to render through devices of illusion and fantasy a meaningless concatenation of events meaningful and rich with purpose?

The only way to approach the answer to this question is to raise the fundamental question of man's nature. If man is a creature whose life is all temporal (a congerie of chemical and biological requirements which make him like to nature and a creature of action and will which make him wholly historical) then, indeed, his life does vanish and pass away, for there is nothing toward which he moves that is not of nature or of history. If such be the case, it may be said that history is transcended only in the memory of man, that the meaning of history lies only in the wisdom with which man learns to accept its decisions, that man—wholly defined by his historicity—transcends it only in the despairing self-awareness that this is all that he can expect, to know the fatality of the historical.

The despairing view of history or the Stoic contentment with the little that can be known does not mean that history is meaningless. It only means that the historian—and every man who asks questions of his own microcosm is a historian of the everyday—comes to his world with a viewpoint which is fashioned out of his own past, his own predilections and disposition, his own character and person. The subjective viewpoint of the historian—whether it be the simple man who wonders about his world or the scholar who investigates a very definite world—presupposes that he stands in an existential relation with the historical, that he be part of history and an acting creature within it. This view, beautifully stated by R. G. Collingwood, is that "to the historian, the activities whose history he is studying are not spectacles to be watched, but experiences to be lived through in his own mind; they are objective, or known to him, only because they are also subjective, or activities of his own." This does not mean that the historian is capricious, that he arbitrarily constructs the past—for the historian can never forget that he is in the present, that the historical event upon which he focuses is past and that he is the medium through whom the past is linked to the future. The historian enables the past to emerge from isolation and be bound to the future. And as the past is transmitted to the future, more of the past is illuminated, because more of the future unfolds the possibility concealed and hidden in the past. It may then be said that only when history is completed will history be known. It is no wonder that early speculation upon the nature of history projected its unity and completion from the point of view of its end.

It is proper at this juncture to distinguish between the end and the meaning of history: it may no longer be possible to speak of the end of history, except by resuscitating an archaic world view; however, we can speak of meaning in pre-apocalyptic terms, as the prophets did, without even placing before ourselves the image of the end. We may restore what early Christianity abolished—the sense that history unfolds through an agonizing dialectic of partial fulfillments and demonic distortions; that as creatures we are confined to the sufficient knowledge of our creatureliness; that any meaning which can be derived from history is realized by man entering the historical moment in search of meaning; and that—for those so blessed by the gift of faith—God reigns over all history. Man is thus finally and unavoidably that unique creature who seeks the meaning of his existence in history.

The problem of history and eschatology may be reconstructed by asserting a number of collateral propositions:

*Historical thinking has for its proper subject matter the whole of human existence.* This is not to say that natural events have no meaningful historical dimension (a natural event which affects the life of man is certainly historical in so far as it affects history, but not in so far as it is natural). At the same moment our definition eliminates from the field of history pure mythologies such as the prehistorical wars of the angels or God's conversations with Satan (except in so far as these mythologies have enabled man to comment and report symbolically upon his own historical condition).

*In historical thinking the thinker not only seizes the object, but the object seizes him—they become intertwined and the thinker is himself involved in the object of thought.* The thinker, in his involvement, seeks to pass beyond the dualism of subject and object; he seeks not to prize or conquer history but to become part of it and by living in and through it to understand it and himself the better. In this manner, when the thinker is also a believer he is placed in a different relation to history. There are certain events which are singled out from the very beginning—events which, though historical themselves, are paradigms of all other historical events. Such sacred events, the giving of the Torah on Sinai for the Jew or the Crucifixion for the Christian, are contemporary events which enable the believer to come to every occasion prepared to discover something in routine history which carries a fulfillment or a reproach to the normative paradigm.

*The purpose of historical thinking is that the thinker enlightens his own existence and, more importantly, that since his existence is in time and itself historical, such thinking enables the thinker to decide for himself how he will live in the future.* Historical thinking enables the existential decision. The relevance of this view to our notion of sacred history is clear: the sacred event is no longer to be taken over whole as it is given. It is first to be freed of its own historical conditioning and disclosed in the nakedness of its teaching. It is then possible for the believing thinker to look to the Bible not as a univocal way—which is to deprive it of its historicity—but as a way for the future, as a possible way for the believing thinker himself. In this manner the Bible becomes transitive, pointing to the future existential decision in which at each moment it is met by the thinker in his own right time and in his own right historical moment. The Biblical event becomes a possible eschatological moment for each thinker. The thinker may negate its relevance, in which case what was opportunity for man becomes disobedience to God. Or the thinker may come to the Biblical event in an attitude of believing reluctance—that is, willingness to believe but a reluctance to authenticate the contemporaneity of the ancient event. Such a thinker will of necessity demythologize the event in order to reveal it (and it is a possibility that to *demythologize* the event is but to *remythologize* it, to divest it of irrelevant myth in order to invest it with relevant myth); he will seek to disclose its essential character in order to incorporate it into his own life. He will convert the closed historical event into the open Word of God. He will thus have transformed the historical into the eschatological, for no longer the causality of the historical (its sources and origins, which are the preoccupations of the scientist of history), but the end and direction of history shall have become his task.

## A Closing Word for the Jews

Judaism has never had to explain a failed eschatology. This is a questionable blessing, for had Judaism been triumphant in the West, its unfulfilled hopes, indeed the reverse, the trampling and despising of its hopes, would not have been as bitter. And yet Judaism has not had power in the West—which is only to say that it has never had the occasion of confusing power with justice or of confusing mercy with the charity of kings. It has continued unfailingly to await the day of the Lord and it has continued to invest that day with a meaning and a finality which is unrelentingly eschatological.

At the same time that Jewish eschatology is spared of past disappointment, its futurity is so absolute that it becomes somewhat vague and bare. The paradox to be sure is here: the Jewish believer must preserve its absolute futurity (to do otherwise is to run the risk of historicizing the *eschaton* as did Rabbi Akiba when he thought to proclaim the messiahship of the heroic Bar Kokhba), but he must also preserve its imminence (to do otherwise is to make his own salvation and that of all history into an abstraction—and salvation is never an abstraction to him who awaits salvation). The eschatological fulfillment which Christianity proclaims and the eschatological futurity which Judaism preserves both have defeating consequences: the former encourages the development of sacred mythologies in order to strengthen and preserve the memory of the past event whose repetition is awaited, while in the latter the forms and structures of past history—which is all that such a believer knows—are falsely eternalized and are gradually substituted for the event to come. In both cases differing mythologies complicate the awareness of the *eschatons*. In the former, mythologies which are drawn down from heaven complicate the image of historical time and in the latter, mythologies which are elicited from the history of man and nations are supernaturalized and compromise trust in the prerogatives of divine action.

The crucial task of the Jew is to keep the *eschaton* as empty of finality as possible while preserving the possibility that each moment might be final. As Martin Buber has observed: "There are no knots in the mighty cable of our Messianic belief, which, fastened to a rock on Sinai, stretches to a still invisible peg anchored in the foundations of the world. In our view, redemption occurs forever, and none has yet occurred. Standing, bound and shackled, in the pillory of mankind, we demonstrate with the bloody body of our people the unredeemedness of the world. For us there is no cause of Jesus; only the cause of God exists for us." The sacred event to which the Jew, reflecting upon history, must turn is the event at Sinai, for in that event the nearness of God was forever made known and, notwithstanding His distance and however He be hidden, He is near at any moment that a man might go forth to hear Him again in his own life and in his own hour.

# The Temper of Jewish
## Anti-Christianity:
# A Theological Statement

THE RELATIONS of Judaism and Christianity from the end of the fourth century, which saw the completion of Jerome's monumental translation of the Hebrew Bible into Latin, until the renewal of Jewish-Christian communication during the nineteenth century were those of compounded ignorance. What had commenced as a struggle in the interest of revealed truth—the quality of that truth and the magnanimity of that revelation—had declined into what can only be regarded as the inheritance, transmission, and renovation of ignorance, each generation forgetting something more about the other, each generation finding in the continued witness of the other some further confirmation for uncharity, suspicion, and hatred. It cannot be denied that my sympathies are with the ignorance which my fellow Jews conserved toward Christianity; however, my sympathies are those of a creature for his fellow creatures, creatures to whom he is bound by the nexus of shared misfortune, for the historical destiny of the nation and people of Israel, construed independently of any role which they may be said to play in the order of salvation, can be only a misfortune. (Would any say that there is glory in having delivered to an unnatural death in the course of two thousand years perhaps as many Jews as are alive today?) On the other hand, if it were my persuasion that my connection to my fellow Jews was but the consequence of historical necessity and unavoidable complicity in their fate, I should be persuaded by reason and good sense to avoid their society and detach myself from their fate. That I might fail in such an undertaking— that, indeed, the likelihood that I would fail may be presumed— would not, of itself, persuade my reason or sway my will not to make the effort. There is, then, no argument from history which would prevent the dissimulation of my origins—my assimilation to anonymity in the Gentile world.

The only grounds on which I may take my stand as a Jew before man and history is that I have been granted no option by God to do otherwise. Though I may elect to be quits with him, to be released from the covenant of my ancestors, it is a release and severance which can follow only from a radical autonomy of will, a suspension of historical realism, a denial of all that in the past which has formed the actual creature who says no. To say no to God—recognizing that it is God to whom one says no—is a fatal contradiction. It is to nullify that which cannot be nullified. The consequence of such an ontologically self-contradictory undertaking is to nullify not God but oneself. If it may be argued that there is no escape possible from the historical condition of the Jew—as a natural-historical phenomenon—it may equally be said that there is no theological exit for the Jew who admits the reality of the God whose very existence authenticates theology. The Jew cannot escape himself. He cannot escape history by entering and disappearing into it. He cannot escape God, for God does not free him. The Jew has no choice but to endure God. It is no less onerous for God to endure the Jew. But it is true, is it not, that a covenant is a covenant. I am, therefore, obliged as a Jew to situ-

ate myself within a curious history—a history which has been
secularized by Christians, although ostensibly redeemed by Christ;
a history in which, as a son of the covenant, I can have no part
in its categories, intentions, fascinations, which are those against
which my ancestors struggled in order to become a Holy People.
In short, the history of times and predicaments, solutions and pro-
visional medicaments is a history in which I participate only to the
extent that I am a man, not to the extent that I am a Jew. To the
extent that I am a Jew all history is an ironic charade or a filmy
gauze through which I dimly see the unfolding of a drama. I do
not comprehend history in my Jewish soul, but I must bear
both its transitory reality and my incomprehension.

## I

It is inappropriate for one such as myself to list the items of
convergence or similarity which might mark the renewal of Jewish-Christian fraternity. Any such dossier of compatibilities would
be essentially unreal, abstract, and hypostatic, encompassing as it
would but the smallest portion of our historical being—for what
we share with Christianity is only our beginnings. It is, however,
what we have built upon our beginnings that describes our disunion; for Judaism, in contrast to Biblical religion, begins at
that moment in which Christianity announces its death, and
Christianity emerges at that moment in which the history of the
Gospels is transformed into the rich categories of Paul the Apostle. The Jew, upon whom the pagan Christian comes to depend for his first knowledge of God, is no longer the lonely, passionate, longing lyricist who is the paradigmatic Jew of the "Old

Testament."[1] He has become, by 70 C.E., certainly by 200 C.E., when Judah the Prince redacts the Mishnah, and surely by the end of the Gaonic era in the tenth century, a creature intent upon sustaining a vision which is finally indifferent to the thrusts and challenges of historical adversaries. The Jew of that advanced time has long since rejected any Jesus who might be the Anointed. The Christian, moreover, is no longer expectant of an imminent parousia. He is, as Eugen Rosenstock-Huessy so tellingly observed to Franz Rosenzweig, no longer in need of any "Old Testament," for after the period of the Councils and the definition of the Creeds and the elaboration of the structure of the Church, the living Christian recalls not the "dead" Jew and his, indeed, *"Old* Testament," but the traditions and witnesses of the early Church which are become his old, that is to say, his historically past witness to the Christ.

The Jew and the Christian, as historical creatures, it would appear, have nothing to say to one another, except in so far as they speak beyond and in spite of faith. But is this really so? Do we not ontologize history too severely by such an affirmation—for if it were true that we have no cause to regard one another, then our continuous historical collision would become more horrendously irrational and our historical alienation even greater cause for despair. Rather, it is the case that we may adduce our continuous historical collision as evidence that we are unable to avoid one another, that our endurance before each other is proof of our

---

1. Throughout this essay I have avoided such commonplace references as Old Testament and the honorific Saint in order to underscore the seriousness of the Jewish-Christian disunion. Moreover, such devices for marking the passage of time in the measurements of Christian anticipation and retrospection are replaced by the usual Jewish nomenclature of C.E. (Common Era) and B.C.E. (Before the Common Era). This is all symbolic usage, but rhetorically appropriate.

interconnection, that in some obscure and indefinite way we are for each other an obligatory testimony.

The vivid presence of Christian to Jew and Jew to Christian is, of course, not reflected in the ballooning expansion of Christianity which transforms it from the faith of individuals redeemed in Jesus Christ into a worldwide institution, which knows few if any of its ancient opponents.

The "foolishness" of the Gospel in the sight of the pagan will pass as the Greek in man languishes before the public and interior victories of the Church.

The pagan may remain unbaptized, but he will no longer be scoffingly indifferent; he will succumb, as do men of the East in our time, to the wisdom of the Gospels, though not yet persuaded of its ultimacy or superiority. But of the stumbling block which the Gospels remain to Israel there can be no alteration, for the imagination of Israel is not peopled with many gods that we should regard the pagan's acknowledgement of Jesus Christ as extraordinary (although we might share with Franz Rosenzweig, to whom we are indebted for this moment of our exegesis, the question of why Jesus Christ and not, as seems often more appropriate, Goethe, Hegel, or Jung). For the pagan, such folly is easily and advantageously remedied; but for Israel that knows from its birth only a single God, to multiply and proliferate him is not only a stumbling block but a meaningless unreality. A messiah, to be sure; a Son of God, hopeless!

The face that Christianity turns toward the world of today is already radiant with triumph. However much it may be subtly corroded by the opposing principalities of state, secular knowledge, and unbelief, it knows that it takes to itself the whole world, that it is in itself the universality which history seeks. The Jew of today, moreover, is no longer the Jew of old, for he is no longer without a shared history, without a participation in the movements and currents of a larger secularity which overwhelm his classic categories of aloofness and encapsulation.

The Jew whose rhythm of time was once marked by a sacral procession of ahistorical events (which were but apparently historical, being in fact the consciously apprehended structures of providence) has disappeared. The Jew of today is permanently postemancipation; he can never again return completely to the precincts of his ancient law. The vast Church and the broken Synagogue—like the figures confronting one another on the façade of the cathedral at Strasbourg—are in our time monuments that become increasingly empty and meaningless, for it matters little whether the Church is vast and universal if Christians have not yet come to the Father, and it does not demean the Synagogue if it is empty as long as there are still Jews frozen in its doorway, seeking to return. Ultimately only individual Christians and individual Jews will form the new community of Church and Synagogue. Divested as we are by history of all that which enabled our participation in a community that could do the will of God with a whole heart, now and for the immediate future, it will only be individual Christians and individual Jews who, in remembrance and recall of their origins, will begin the renewal.

The Church, triumphant over history in the universality of the Johannine Gospel, is victor and loser, for its commitment to historical structures and inherited dominions makes it partner to precisely the history which it seeks to annihilate. The Jew, the victim of history, renounces the eternity he carries within him in order that he may share, not the universality of world history, but the *worldliness* of world history in the renascent nationalism of the Jewish people. In sum, therefore, it may be said that the externally apprehended Jew provided the occasion and the rationalization for the attachment of Christian faith to precisely that history which, in its origins, it was obliged to refuse; and the conduct of the

Christian toward the Jew provided the occasion for the Jewish refusal of its vocation to the Christian—the rejection of the Christ by the Jews compelling Christianity into world history and consecrating it to the often bloody task of "saving" whole nations and peoples; the persecution of the Jew forcing Judaism to seek the succor and favor of any and all neutral and antipathetic powers of this world by which to mitigate and contain the enmity of Christianity.

Our historical collision is, therefore, the consequence of defective understanding, a default of mutuality, a refusal to acknowledge that though the Father may be One and solitary, his providence remains a mystery, perhaps the only authentic mystery for time and history.

## II

We return, as we must, to the primary question: what does the Jew say of Jesus as the Christ? For, indeed, what I have observed above would not have come to be if the Jews in the time of Jesus of Nazareth had acknowledged his messiahship.

We shall not rehearse the narrative of historical events—that only a small number of Jews knew of Jesus' claim to be the Christ; that Judaism was already by the time of Jesus a religion diffused throughout the Roman world, numbering one in ten Roman citizens as full or partial converts; that Jewish leadership, extraordinarily harassed as it was by Roman authority, behaved, in spite of the trial and condemnation of Jesus, with remarkable indifference toward him, regarding him less as a falsely intentioned insurrectionist than as another of the pretender messiahs of whom tradition records that seventy appeared and seventy were condemned and executed; that Jewish messianism, although profound, was heavily scarred by mythological construction, being imprecise, vague, and fundamentally undisciplined. It might be said that Jesus was, so far as the Palestinian Judaism of the first century is concerned, a religious eccentric whose doctrine and practice had politically debilitating side effects. He was paid little attention by the Jews of his day; and, given the unremitting efforts of Christendom for two millennia to enforce the attention of the Jew, it must be remarkable and disconcerting to Christian missionaries to observe how little attention he is paid by Jews even today.

Such historical derogation, however accurate it might be for the brief period which encloses the actual life of Jesus of Nazareth, is immediately transformed by the events which succeed his death. It is one thing to judge in the moment of apparition the truth or untruth of an historical person, to condemn or acquit, to praise or to curse; it is quite another when the generations which succeed such persons insist upon recalling, remembering, testifying, and transmitting the knowledge of his life, works, and death. At such moments memory transforms the historical person, informing him with a context and association which indeed he may not have enjoyed, adjudicating and appraising his significance, radiating his influence into cultures and societies of which he knew nothing, connecting and relating what he said in some isolated sector of the world to all that the world was saying at that moment. How much more so is the case when the memory conserves, not simply ordinary persons but prophets or saints, crystallizing and freezing events of the life past into examples and testimonies for the instruction of the future; and how much more still, how unbelievably much more when a few disciples incorporate every word, every gesture, every activity of the person and elevate these into no less than a God who assumed the aspect of mortality and a mortal who was himself the perfect incarnation of God. When such happens—and it has happened but once—the past is sundered from that moment of his contemporaneity and the future is become like to nothing which has been or could be before. This, in essence, is what has been accomplished by the Synoptic Gospels. But it was not sufficient. The Petrine Church, the community of Jewish Christians, who were knowing and obedient to the Torah, might well have come to be regarded by regnant Jewry as heresy and schism to be calmly fought and as calmly returned in penitence to the Synagogue—for the Pharisees were not unsympathetic to the advent of the messiah, and they were familiar with the passion to consummation which seethed in their own time. That they judged Jesus to be false was inescapable; but that his disciples judged Jesus—in spite of continued eschatological disappointment and postponement—to be still true, is yet (however much a misjudgment in my sight) a continuing source of wonder and bafflement, as it is that in the years following his death there should arise one who, persuaded to belief, turned the entire force of his intellectual skill to the creation of a theology to interpret disappointment, a theology which at the same time could address the anguish of the pagan in terms which made the disappointment of the parousia not only believable but its chief power and strength.

It is, therefore, for me, a Jew, as much a mystery that Christianity survived and triumphed as it is a mystery for Christianity that the unconverted Jew persists, not only in his unbelief but in the confident assertion that he is still chosen by God, covenanted to him, and patient before his ultimate discretion.


### III

Even if the death of Jesus of Nazareth is without significance for Israel in its own understanding of salvation, the fact remains that as long as history accounts that death as being more, as the death not of a carpenter from Nazareth but of Jesus the Christ, then Israel cannot but entertain that historical fact as though it were *more* than history. Believing it, however, to be no more than history and knowing it as history, Israel must conjure with what this means for those who affirm it as an action of God, that is, as a fact whose meaning exceeds the plane of the historical. Israel must soften its heart before the historical happening of the life and death of Jesus for the sake of those who affirm it to be more than history; but, likewise, those who believe in Jesus as the Christ and in their belief know its truth for themselves, must understand what is affirmed in Jewish unbelief.

The unbelief of Israel, as it regards Jesus Christ, is the belief of Israel in God who himself is, does, and works all things. That we do not believe in Jesus as the Christ is for the fact that we believe in God; and were it that we believe not in our true belief, surely then we could not believe in him who is believed by Christians to come from God himself. Therefore the unbelief of Israel in Jesus as the Christ is not unbelief in God (for God could have worked in Jesus of Nazareth, all things being possible to God). It is only that the Jew—who is saved by God himself, being with him from his own birth—is not saved by him who came after for the sake of those who were born after. Israel's belief makes possible that the nations shall believe in Jesus Christ, but that Jesus Christ shall save them is only for the fact that Israel is not yet saved. In that consummate time all men shall be saved in fact, whereas now we are saved only in that we believe in God and in believing do his *mitzvot* (commandments) and in doing his *mitzvot* obey his will. Our obedience is to the Law of God, whether that Law be for the Gentiles in Jesus Christ or in the Torah of Israel.

## IV

Having affirmed the historical disjunction of Jew and Christian, we are still obliged to address ourselves to the vastly more thorny issue, not of Jewish rejection in the time of Jesus Christ or the formation of a theology by which rejection and unbelief are transformed into service and fidelity, but rather of how, in the face of history, Jewish rejection has not only continued but strengthened and become emboldened.

I shall not examine the fundamental opposition of Torah and Jesus Christ, for that issue, central though it is to my thought, requires a different approach independent of the one we have defined. Let me present my view by responding to two passages in which Thomas Aquinas expands on Paul's Epistle to the Romans (chapter 3).[2]

> The New Law is not disjunct from the Old Law, because they have both the same end, namely, man's subjection to God; and there is but one God of the New and the Old Testaments, according to Romans 3:29-31: "Or is God the God of Jews only? Is he not the God of Gentiles also? Yes, of Gentiles also, since God is one; and he will justify the circumcised on the ground of their faith and the uncircumcised through their faith. Do we then overthrow the law by this faith? By no means! On the contrary, we uphold the Law." The unity of faith under both Testaments witnesses to the unity of end. . . . Yet faith had a different state in the Old and New Law, since what they believed as future, we believe as fact.

2. *Summa Theologiae*, parts i, ii, qu. 107, art 1; qu. 104, art 2, Reply to Second Objection.

COMMENT I. In Romans 3:9, Paul affirms that all men, both Jews and Greeks, are under the power of sin. If all men are equally condemned before God, then surely there can be no difference between the Torah and Jesus Christ other than that the Torah promises the inheritance of the future, while the Christian announces salvation as accomplished. The ransom from sin which the Christ affords is given, but the "ransom" which the Torah affords becomes illusory. Before the judgment of God, imminent as it is, no man can be patient. While the Torah is turned to the future, damnation is at hand. This is a persuasive rhetoric to unhappy Romans who knew not what it was the Torah promised, but knew too well what it was their hour demanded.

The critical misapprehension is that the Law does not promise salvation, nor was it ever thought to promise it. The Law is but the Way to the Father; it is the structure which allows disordered life to be educated. The Law is holy culture (and thus, as Denis de Rougemont noted, impoverished in all the familiar artifices of culture),[3] but culture is not and never was a substitute for the Messiah. The Law is propaedeutic to redemption but is no substitute for it. It is the container and corrective to sin; it does not ransom from sin. It is the inspiriter and director of right action, but it is not righteousness itself. The radicalization of alternatives before the common human condition of sinfulness is one upon which Paul capitalizes in his witness to the pagan. It is irrelevant to the Jew.

COMMENT II. The mystery of Israel to the nations is that it regards the gift of the Anointed to the pagan as a fortuity in no way integral to the life of Israel. This position is logically comprehen-

3. Denis de Rougemont, "The Vocation and Destiny of Israel," *The Christian Opportunity*, Holt, Rinehart and Winston, New York, 1963, p. 59 f.

sible and meaningful only if the messianism of Israel is tied to the End, the real End. For Israel there can be no penultimates. If there are penultimate ends, caesuras and breaks in the unfolding of history toward salvation, then our first rejection of Jesus as Christ shall have been as much an error as would be our rejection of a second or a third or an indefinite number of messiahs, whose advent brings no End. If the Christ returns and the End is not with his coming, then surely Israel is justified in its first refusal; but if he comes again and with his coming there is the true and consummate End and Israel again refuses, then surely Israel is condemned, for what is presently futurity and expectation in our sight becomes at that time the reckless refusal of salvation. We shall not, I pray, refuse to believe then, at that distant moment to come, for in believing *then* amid the conclusion of history, we shall have justified our unbelief past, and if we do not believe at the true End, we shall have demonstrated that our earlier unbelief was already our condemnation. This judgment is to God alone and neither to us nor to the Paul of Romans 3.

> The Jewish People were chosen by God that the Christ might be born of them. Consequently the entire state of that people had to be prophetic and figurative, as Augustine states. For this reason even the judicial precepts that were given to this people were more figurative than those which were given to other nations. Thus, too, the wars and deeds of this people are expounded in the mystical sense; but not the wars and deeds of the Assyrians and Romans, although the latter are more famous in the eyes of men.

It is hopeless to expect that this view of Thomas Aquinas, a view already well expounded by Paul, should be received by Jewish tradition with anything more than uncomprehending anger or amazement. Indeed, Jewish reaction could be no less conclusive than that of Nietzsche when he observed in his *Morgenröte*:

"The Christians gave themselves up to a passion for reinterpretation and substitution—a process which cannot possibly have been compatible with good conscience. However much Jewish scholars protested, it was affirmed that everywhere in the Old Testament the theme was Christ and only Christ." It must be acknowledged, however, that strictures against the Pauline typological construction of the Hebrew Bible are legitimated only on the presumption that Jesus is not the Christ. The violence which Paul does to the scriptural narrative of the life of Abraham, or the person of Moses, or to the prophecies of Isaiah and Jeremiah is violence in two senses. First, the exegetic rendering is a forcing and misconstruction of the actual text (that is to say, it is a literary mishandling of texts whose Jewish principles of exegesis, always more explicit and reasonable in its use of *peshat, derash, remez* and *sod*,[4] are to be deplored). Second, his notion of divine foreshadowing and divine concealment by which the Hebrew Bible does become, indeed, the "old" and the past covenant preparing man and history for the new is a violence to the reality of Jewish faith.

Let us grant the exigencies which compelled Paul to this exegetic turn: the necessity of bringing the promise of salvation to the Gentiles, the equivalence which he felt obliged to establish between the Gentile in Christ and the born Jew, and finally the confirmation of the rejection of the Jewish people, the Torah, and the modalities of Jewish redemption in order that the missionary appeal of Judaism to the pagan world be blunted and the superiority of Christianity be defined. All Pauline judgments are understandable if the situation of the young Church amid the Gentiles

4. The traditional modes of Rabbinic exegesis are *peshat* as the simple, literal meaning of a word or passage; *derash* as the exegesis by homiletic parallelism and analogy; *remez* as symbolic meaning; *sod* as mystical exegesis.

and the conflict of the Church of the Gentiles with the Jerusalem Church and with the rather appealing views of the Ebionites are regarded as the background of Paul's typological derogation of Judaism. Paul was waging a struggle within the Church; and the more intense the struggle became, the more radical became his polarization of the Torah, Judaism, Israel, and the Christ.

On any objective grounds it is hopeless to inquire whether Paul reads the Bible correctly: he reads it correctly if one is a Christian who may say in faith that all is possible to God, even the use of the generations from Adam to Abraham to Jesus the Christ as preliminary and preparatory to the regeneration and salvation of man. To the Jew, however, what Thomas Aquinas takes for granted is senseless.

COMMENT I. If the Jew is without faith in that which is prefigured in his Bible but believes rather that what he is given in Scripture is to be understood as God speaks it and gives it, then to make retrospectively of God a figural revealer is to seal into the faith of the Christian and the responding faith of the Jew an abiding and immutable incomprehension.

The true speech between Christian and Jew, the only speech possible against the background of figural, allegorical, and typological exegesis, is that of the masked dialogue in which each word spoken can be understood only as its opposite; for that which the Christian speaks of the Jew, the Christian speaks literally (since he, in fact, speaks of the Christ come in whom he believes), while the Jew hears such speech figurally as the anticipation of him who is yet to come. When the Jew, on the other hand, speaks to the Christian of the Torah, meaning that this Torah is the Way before the future, the Christian hears the Law figurally as the incompleteness and adumbration of him who has come.

In effect, the Christian reads futurity back into the past, and the Jew ontologizes the past before the future. The Christian, from his perspective, cannot help but mythologize a reality which in its *real* existence is prophecy outlined, consummated, and thereby petrified if it survives beyond its fulfillment; for that reality is to the Christian the old covenant which has indeed ended and, moreover, never really existed as the Jews believe it to exist, since its function was always prophetic and thus always a future for the present, a future event even at the moment of the giving of the Law, the building of the Temple, or the instruction of the prophets.

The movement from Paul's epistolary halfway house for Israel, to the Letter of Barnabas in which the existence of any covenant between God and Israel is repudiated, to the doctrine of Marcion that the God of the Jews is "an alien God" is henceforward a reasonably easy one. Paul takes Israel seriously, but it is an Israel in which no Jew believed. The Israel of Paul is a theological construction and a theological necessity; it is an intermediate device which must be employed that the pagan world be redeemed in Christ—at which point, hopefully, in the spirit of Romans, God might return to graft on once more the broken shoots of the old stock of Israel. Israel is for Paul and for the Christian the first thought and the last, but the middle is all of Christ. Such a use of the presence of Israel cannot be less than a falsehood in our sight.

COMMENT II. The requirement of Pauline eschatology, implicit in the observation of Thomas Aquinas, is that the Jew is become a chimera, a substantial chimera but nonetheless a shadow creature enduring a shadow history. If the Jew endures beyond the fulfillment of his own prophecy, then his perduration can only be construed as a divine witness of judgment. God preserves the Jew as threat to the Christian and testimony to the bankruptcy

47

of the Jew. The Jew becomes a myth in so far as any reality he enjoys unto himself becomes irrelevant. What comes to count is his hypostatic, exemplary existence as a dismembered, dispersed, and condemned people. But such a view has serious consequences for the manner in which Jew and Christian, Synagogue and Church view one another now, nearly two millennia after the fact, when we are become no longer dogmatic enemies but common seekers of the truth.

The Christian has been obliged by his tradition either to naturalize or demonize the Jew: to naturalize him in so far as the Jew no longer resembles the Jew of the myth, to demonize him in so far as the Jew continues to resemble the Jew of the myth. The Jew, on the other hand, either naturalizes or demonizes the power of the Church: naturalizing it in so far as its power is regarded as no different than any other center of authority in a secular society; demonizing it in so far as the Church, in fidelity to its theological origins in Paul, must regard the Jew as continuing testimony to its own, the Church's failure. There is, however, a deeper level to the mutual mythologies which we entertain. Christian and Jew cannot avoid mythologizing each other because each can only know the external function the other performs within the closed system of his truth. Can I, for example, regard the Christian as other than an errant, misguided believer—a believer who believes within a universe that rebukes the substance of his belief? (For my eyes, in my unbelief, cannot see the redemption which he sees; and his eyes, in his belief, cannot know the quality of continuing unredeemedness.) The Jew mythologizes the *goy* (the Gentile, the individual among the nations who knows not the God of Israel), for he cannot help but regard his supernatural vocation in the Church as but a mask for the palpable unfulfillment and incompletion of Christianity; for the Christ did not yet return, as he believed in the infancy of his faith he would, and the objective time and history which we share as Christian and

Jew is unredeemed. Similarly, the Christian mythologizes the Jew either by declining to regard his existence beyond 70 C.E. as other than a fortuity, *or* as a mystery by which God declines, for reasons inscrutable, to consummate his promise in Jesus Christ by ending history and converting the Jews, *or* as a historical scandal to the Church, for the continuance of the Jew is mute testimony that the Christ has not yet come for all the universe, that the pagan is not yet ransomed from his superstition, and that the Jews—not a remnant, not the witness of a handful, but a whole community—persist in its way, ignoring the Church of Christ.

Does it not finally seem, therefore, in so far as the parousia is still before us, that Christian eschatology is unfulfilled, that Jewish eschatology is yet unrealized, that we are, both Jew and Christian, in the same human and historical predicament? Our common promise is behind us; our common hope is before us. There is no difference between the Jesus of the Gentiles and the Torah of the Jews—no functional difference as regards the End—although there are crucial and decisive differences which emerge relative to our distance from the End.


## V

Having affirmed, rather incompletely and obliquely, I am afraid, the utter divergence of the view of Israel and the view of the Church regarding the event of Jesus as Christ, we are nevertheless obliged to live with one another in the same world. How can it be, we may ask, that God apparently cherishes our disagreement? For we would not have endured in separateness for two millennia, preserving as we do the distinctive modes of our existence before each other and before the rest of the world, had it not been that he finds a use in our encounter. Part of the answer is surely that the End has not come, that history is not yet perfected into the Kingdom and beneath the Kingship of God, that mankind is still suffering from the bite of that primordial serpent, the tempter and the adversary of God.

*We are removed from one another in faith:* our putative Pelagianism which affirms that all is in the hand of heaven, excepting the fear of heaven is surely removed from the Christian view that the endowments of faith are the gift of God. *We are surely removed in practice:* though Judaism always runs the risk of decaying into a foolish formalism, it *does* still believe that God has vouchsafed us an instruction by which to make ourselves fearers and lovers of his person (the Law in this regard being viewed by innumerable rabbinic sources as the *via media* which nourishes and guides and directs our natural knowledge of God into our supernatural awe and love); the Christian holds that the Law is only a substitute for the *Kyrios Christos*, a preparatory stage to be transcended and abrogated. For us our works count before God—not the stated commandments only (for the commandments explicate what we might not have known to do without revelation), but the commandments which all of the literature of Israel regards as being written in the heart of man; for the Christian, works tend to count for rather less than faith—and I might well sympathize with such a heterodox emphasis, for I find the articles of Christian faith so scandalously demanding that, not unlike Paul judging that the Law cannot be kept, I wonder at the extent and perfectness of any possible Christian faith. *We are removed from one another in our understanding of divinity:* for us there is but God alone and he is unique, capable of all those works of charity, grace, and redemption for which the Christian requires the mediation of the Incarnation. Can a Jew ever understand the Incarnation other than as a typology in reverse—as an analogy wherewith to instruct the Gentiles by vivid image and living symbol what it is that Torah asks of man? *We are distant from one another in our view of man:* we regard him as the creature of his Creator, distant and near to him, imperfect before a criterion of perfection which is the Image in which he was created, victim of temptation and impulse, victor in that he subdues and orders his passion, neither evil beyond measure nor good beyond credibility. Man, to whom Torah is given, is the *benoni*, neither saint nor monster, and it is for him that the world is sometimes thought to have been created. Such a view of man (a realistic humanism, I believe) is at odds with the radical human predicament which Paul and later Marcionite tendencies (never properly or successfully overcome within the Church) describe. Man had to be in total bondage to sin that the extraordinary challenge of the Christ might seem appropriate; moreover, he had to pass through eons of regeneration before Christ could return in order that the fact that he did not return promptly could be sustained. The anthropology of Christianity is, I fear, an anthropology which unless corrected—and I believe profoundly corrected —by Biblical humanism cannot but fail, for it was an anthropology appropriate to the period immediately succeeding the death of Jesus, but is hopeless for a humanity that has none of the chiliastic opportunities of the monk, solitary, or ascetic in which to withdraw, but must—like the Jew—maintain the whole of the religious life while earning bread, raising a family, building a home, and waiting for the Messiah.

## VI

We are left with a perplexity. I have virtually stated throughout that I do not believe in the Judeo-Christian tradition. I regard this conception as an ideologizing of a fundamental and irreconcilable disagreement. There is a Jewish-Christian nexus; there is a Jew for the Christian and there is a Christian for the Jew, but the reciprocity of their relation arises, not from the assumption of their communality, but from the assumption of their difference. The nexus is that Christian and Jew divide before the same Lord; it is the sameness of the Lord which establishes our connection, but it is the breach of our understanding of him that makes all use of the significant word "tradition" hopelessly irrelevant.

There is indeed a "carrying over" from Jew to Christian; in that sense there is a Judeo-Christian tradition, a tradition determined by the Christian's dependence upon the Jew for his past. But this hyphenated tradition is not reversible. There is no Christo-Jewish tradition, no passage backward, no return into us except in the fullness of days. It is not incorrect to say that to the extent that we begin in this time to communicate anew with Christians as believers who believe differently, but seek to learn from us in truth what it is that has sustained us during the centuries that have elapsed since the time the Church cut us off in our living members and refashioned us as a Christian myth, we may be beginning the joint work of coredemption to which I have alluded.

Confessional conversation between Jew and Christian only takes place when two persons who are really connected address each other, when they acknowledge their sharing of a history but believe it to signify different truths, when both direct their energies to the transformation of the same humanity and the same past. In this sense Jew and Christian are empirically equals, although their equality under nature and history is differently quantified by the roles and attitudes and postures which their historical past has enforced upon their contemporary views of each other. But they also meet each other at a different plane, for when they eliminate from their views the mockeries of history—when the Christian overcomes his terrestrial fear of the Jew and when the Jew deadens the pain of his historical encounter with Christendom—then there is the possibility of asking what claim each makes upon the other. I do not mean the claim of each turned outward to the world but looking back over the shoulder toward the other; rather, what claim each directly makes upon the other, and is it a significant claim?

The Christian is present for the Jew only as a reminder of that which the Jew must expect and as a witness to what he has been allowed to forego in order that the pagan world might be redeemed. The Christian is the visible testimony for the Jew of his messianic vocation, that he never be permitted to throw off what only he, as Jew, can do, which is to affirm that amid the cry of all, there is still no peace—even more, that there is no *shlamut*, no perfection until Christianity is reunited with Israel, until it has learned to transcend the Son to the Father, until it too shall have learned to say Lord and Lord alone, having been instructed to do so by the Son.

We await patiently the return of Christendom to the Synagogue, as we await patiently the coming of the messianic herald of the End; but we do so not with the trumpet of the missionary nor the timbrel of the tract—for it is a requirement that the only proselyte who comes wholly within our gate be one who has learned of his own to love and fear God, and loving and fearing him seeks then to serve him. So we are patient before the reunion. Can we be more than patient before the reunion? What more has Israel to offer the world than an eternal patience?

# Two Views of the Church:
## The Natural and the
## Supernatural Jew

THE CONCEPTS of the natural and the supernatural Jew are inescapably dialectical. They are inescapably dialectical because they are concepts which arise from reflection upon the nature and process of history.

The natural Jew is a historical phenomenon—born in the eighteenth century, nourished in the nineteenth, triumphant in the twentieth. The fact that the modern Jew is a creature of emancipation—that his Jewishness is but one among his attributes, rarely superior to others, characteristically an equal among equals—does not destroy the theological validity of holding that whatever his commitment to the order of nature and history, the Jew participates, by definition as does the Christian, in a sacred order of history. The sacred dimension of history—that dimension which was adumbrated by Joseph when he informed his brothers that what they had intended for evil God had construed for good—accentuates the insistence that history is interpenetrated by the divine; that however the divine be indifferent to the efforts of proof and demonstration, it is nevertheless open to the confirmation of faith. It would be impossible to demonstrate that the Red Sea parted for the Children of Israel, but it is fitting and proper for faith to construe such fortuity as miraculous. If indeed the natural event coincided with the demand of history; if the Sea did part at that moment when history required its parting, the faithful may adjudge it miraculous. Sacred history is open to the reading of faith—it is a coincidence of human anguish, the unfolding of providence, and the exegesis of faith.

The natural Jew is to be seen against the background of secular history—his Judaism consists in the influences which the history of the Jewish people has brought to bear upon him. They are natural influences—the influences of historical experience, tradition, culture. They are little different in substance or quality from the generalizations which we allow ourselves (with more or less accuracy) concerning Germans, Frenchmen, or Russians. When, however, the history of the Jew is seen from the view of faith, when it is constructed against the background of the Word of God, a different Jew emerges. The supernatural Jew is he who lives before the background of a limbo-history, a history fashioned in the obscure conversations of God and a motley congregation of wanderers in the Sinai desert. This history—out of which has been fashioned a community and for which God has appointed a destiny—is then to be contrasted, most fruitfully, with other supernatural communities. Its reality and its claim are placed in apposition, not to the natural Jew or the natural European, but to the supernatural Christian. In the same measure as the supernatural Jew may transcend history to God, so may the supernatural Christian. It would have been well if, in the course of Western history, both Jew and Christian had acknowledged the complementary character of their religious vocations. This has not been the case. The Christian has accorded another station to the Jew—a station of incompletion and inadequacy. To the

Christian the Jew is but a frozen community, paralyzed by error, incapsulated by its own self-deceptions.

What I propose to investigate are the two views with which the Jew confronts the Christian world: the view of the natural Jew—liberal, secular intellectual, a latter-day caricature of the minor prophets—and the supernatural Jew, who is legatee of an admittedly unfulfilled but by no means superseded community. The Jew confronts, however, not Christendom *in extenso,* not the Christian community, but the Catholic Christian Church. I have chosen to see the Jew over against Catholic Christianity for the reason that Catholicism has, as a church claiming apostolic succession and insisting upon the primacy of its Patristic tradition, both close historical connections with the Jewish community since the Fall of the Temple and an apologetic relationship which has never ended.

Protestant consideration of Judaism has either been the red-hot irrationalism of Luther's anti-Judaism (which owed much to the historical attitude of German Catholicism) or the sentimentality of much contemporary Protestantism—which would either abandon the whole argument (as Reinhold Niebuhr has suggested) or continue a kind of enthusiastic evangelization that would be unspeakably vulgar if it were not so incredibly unhistorical and ineffectual.

I address myself primarily to the Catholic Christian and the Catholic Church because it alone has maintained a continuing tradition of both historical animus and the sophistication of theological argument. The same generation which saw the Catholic Primate of Poland, Cardinal Hlond, urge in 1936 the strengthening of anti-Jewish legislation witnessed as well Jacques Maritain's writing of the "mystery of Israel." The Catholic Church has a position which stands in contrast and opposition to that of the Jew. The position of the supernatural Jew emerges most clearly when seen against the background of Catholic argument. Moreover, the continuing role and destiny of the Jewish community as a religious community is only to be defined against the background and in response to the affirmations of Christianity, for it alone has fashioned our present historical condition.

It should not surprise reflective Catholics to discover that Jews are, by and large, suspicious—if not openly hostile—toward the Catholic Church. Assuredly it does not surprise Jews to acknowledge the general, however tranquilized, anti-Semitism (anti-Judaism) of most Catholics.

Catholic anti-Semitism is directed to a secular image of the Jewish people. This is perhaps as it should be, for Judaism is but the name by which a holy community—a people—passed into the modern world. Judaism *is not* a religion; the Jewish people *has* a religion. The Catholic anti-Semite no longer links the medieval image of the theological recusant with the modern conception of the Jew. The modern anti-Semite builds his image of the Jew upon the foundations of industrial and urban society. The Jew is no longer conceived as simple unbeliever—he is unbeliever with wealth, power, and disproportionate influence or else alienated, resentful, and *declassé*. In either case the modern image of the Jew no longer depends upon the lineaments of theological argument. The modern anti-Semite owes more, one might say, to the language of Marx's youthful *Zur Judenfrage* than he does to the medieval discourses of Abner of Burgos, Geronimo de Santa Fé, or Paul of Burgos. The former is consequential to the secularization of society—in which the Jew was (as all of us) both emancipated and enslaved; the latter addressed a well-organized society in which Jews were not, for all their disability and suffering, anonymous. The modern anti-Semite is only incidentally Catholic. His Catholicism is only a tributary source of his anti-Semitism. It may afford him an illicit species of rationalization, but such makes his anti-Semitism all the more reprehensible. It is noteworthy that he is not anti-Jewish, but anti-Semitic. He is against the "race," not the people; he reviles a fiction, not a reality.

The Jew, by contrast, is suspicious of the Church. Not the individual but the Church bears the onus of his suspicion. The formulations of Jewish anti-Catholicism do not center upon the social or economic power of the individual Catholic, but upon the real and imagined power of the Church. Indeed if one brings to judgment the actions of the Visible Church—whatever one's casuistry and the subtlety of one's distinctions—the Visible Church may be accounted guilty. We need not rehearse the historical anguish of the Jewish people amid the Christian nations of Europe. It is a record of exclusion, disability, dislocation, and death. More Jews have been slain in the twenty centuries of Jewish dispersion than were slain by Hitler. We should not ascribe it to the merit of history that what Hitler accomplished in but few years the West had the forbearance to spread thinly over centuries. The result is the same: the House of Israel can only remember the injustice of the human and fallible fellowship of Christian believers. It might be imagined that as assimilation takes its course Jews would forget the wound of history. It is, however, the irony of Jewish destiny and an adumbration of its divinity that where Jews have forgotten all—all belief, all conviction, all practice— they remember the outrage of history. One might surmise that it is this outrage—perhaps more than all else—which drove them to forgetfulness, which accelerates their passage from belief to unbelief. To deny is to forget—yet, in the end, what impels denial cannot be forgotten. The pain of Jewish history is the last to disappear. Indeed, it refuses to be vanquished.

The natural Jew is reminded by history that he cannot erase the mark of supernatural destiny. As natural Jew—divested of supernatural motive and intention—he still comes before the Church in questioning incredulity.

## I. The Natural Jew and the Social Image of the Church

The Catholic Church appears to the natural Jew to exemplify many failings, not the least of which is her failure to live up to the world's image of her avowed perfection.

The liberal intellectual (and the natural Jew is often a liberal intellectual) no longer enjoys the privileged position which he once occupied. Liberalism (however this vague term be understood) does not commend itself with the ring of youth and optimism which it possessed three decades ago. The liberal is a believer without a movement, a party, or a cause. Where, until quite recently, one spoke with mocking sadness of "disenchanted radicals," it has become commonplace now to speak of disenchanted liberals. The disenchantment is not a judgment on liberal convictions, but on liberal effectiveness. The liberal is singularly impotent. The response of impotence is often to acquire power. This is rarely a bold and self-conscious gesture. It is more likely to be carried on under the disguise of critical attention to the power held by others.

The liberal need not join the Catholic Church to feel himself competent to judge it. Where, in the thirties, the Left criticized the Church *de rigueur*, as part of an organized program of undermining "the conspirators of reaction," it has now become common for liberals to confront the Church with its own doctrine, to attend to its obtuseness in the political order, to question its judgment or practice in international affairs. This peculiar attention of the liberal mind to the conduct of the Church is intriguing for its lack of bitterness, for its intrinsic respect and thinly veiled admiration. The Church is somehow seen as the single, coherent international power capable of concretizing many of the values which liberals have been advocating for generations, if not centuries. The Church, a conservative institution, has caught up to liberal ideas—its social doctrine is sufficiently advanced to be confusing even to Congressional investigators of un-American ideologies.

The liberal fascination with the Church, the willingness of numerous non-Catholic intellectuals to criticize with partisan affection the conduct of the Church is, however, indication of a more profound *malaise*: a misconstruction of the Church in history and a surrender of the liberal mind, not to faith, but to power. The readiness with which papal teaching on communism, social movements, psychoanalysis is scanned and manipulated by such intellectuals is clear demonstration of a misuse of the Church and a despair of independent effectiveness except through alignment with existing power. Moreover, when the Church performs "ill" or fails to perform, it is treated to strenuous criticism. Presumably the Church has "betrayed" itself, sacrificed its Christian teaching to expediency. Thus the consistent pacifist criticism of the Church's reluctance to speak unambiguously on the use of atomic weapons or on Vietnam.

Ramon Sender, writing in the anti-Franco journal *Iberica*, commented: ". . . one fact stares us in the face with sad eloquence: wherever the Catholic Church is predominant, there is poverty." Sender grants that St. Thomas, and centuries later Leo XIII, acknowledged that material security was indispensable for the exercise of virtue; yet he adds that Leo XIII published his encyclicals many years after the First and Second International had begun to wage the struggle for better working conditions in Europe. The implication is that the Church had correct teaching, but failed to use its moral and political power to effectuate it. A further implication is that the Church always does too little and too late.[1]

To cite another example, many Jews expect the contemporary Church to make amends for its historical hostility to the Jew. It should not be held against the Jew that history has prevented him from drawing theological distinctions which, to his lights, seem irrelevant and unavailing. It is extremely difficult for Jews to understand such distinctions as that between the Visible and Invisible Church; nor would I warrant that such distinctions make particular sense to me. The fact remains that if one view the Church from the outside, such of its figures as Saint Vincent Ferrer or John of Capistrano strike one as peculiarly anomalous: praised for their sanctity and devotion yet notorious for their anti-Jewish agitation. It cannot be asked that Jews judge with sophistication and charity when history has conditioned them to neither. It makes no sense to the Jew that the Visible Church is held by Catholics to be accountable and guilty, whereas the Invisible Church continues to manifest the purity of the Mystical Body. The Jew seeks the solicitude of the Church, not from the justification of theological charity, but from the secular tradition of liberalism of which many modern Jews are ardent spokesmen. The confusion of ancestry, Mosaic ethical doctrine, and secular liberalism produces an amalgam which yields to misconstruction of the Church and its role. A theologically trained Jew, who knows how Jewish law and practice was formed, would not be so impatient with the apparent immobility and dispassion of the Church.

Underlying the attitude of Ramon Sender, the natural Jew I have presented, or other liberal intellectuals whom one might cite, is the conviction that the Church can act but does not; has

1. The debate generated by Rolf Hochhuth's play, *The Deputy*, centered about much the same criticism.

the power to command attention and obedience in areas of social and political policy, and desists. For the man of action (and most liberals see themselves as active, not speculative, men) the practical behavior of the Church is simply not intelligible.

I do not wish to raise the question of the conditions under which the Pope speaks; when and how he speaks; the distinctions which define his pronouncements of doctrine and his statements of opinion; the obligations his words carry. Such questions are not of moment here. What is of importance is the psyche that underlies the attitude of those who, standing outside the Church, nevertheless expect the Church to fulfill the world for them, to transform it by her power, turn its moral force to their service—in effect, to live up to their image of her perfection and strength.

It is patently clear that many liberals are trapped by the ambiguity of their respect for and equally passionate mistrust of power. At the same moment as they would insist that the removal, effected by the Treaty of Westphalia, of papal intervention in secular and political affairs be maintained, they seek such intervention when it supports their own secular and political allegiances. As frequently as liberals would praise papal intervention they would oppose it. It is clear that, in the main, they are not willing to pay the full price for papal commitment and involvement in the temporal order—they would have it only on their terms. Within the orbit of power they are justified in their selective approval of papal intervention, but they should be equally ready to countenance—as they are usually not—that the papacy may, on given issues, be unwilling or unable to cooperate with their objectives.

Fundamentally the non-Catholic intellectual tends to see the Church, not as a religious institution, but as an instrument of power. Since there is so little coherent, organized, and efficient power in the world capable of combatting "alien" ideologies with ideological weapons, the Church is called upon to fill this role. It is considered of little importance that the Church has a tradition and doctrine shaped by theological convictions of patience, providence, and divine grace that are not always responsive to the demands of the moment. What is apparent is that it has power. The plea is for the Church to act regardless of doctrine or situation, to use its power of excommunication against all kinds of evildoers, whether Fascists, Francoists, Communists, practicers of genocide, advocates of nuclear warfare and preventive wars. I do not deny that, in theory, such exercise of power would be desirable. If, indeed, by simple threat of excommunication warmakers could be enjoined and potential murders deflected, there might be merit in the exercise of such power.

Such a position is based, however, on three obvious fundamental misconstructions of the Church: it assumes first, that the Church is all of time and history; second, that the Church can control by the exercise of power alone the course of historic forces; and third, that moral power, independent of community, can accomplish a transformation of heart and head.

The Church, to the extent that it views itself as a supernatural institution, is both of eternity and time. It is in history, but not of history. Whether the non-Catholic believes this to be true or not, it assuredly affects the manner in which the Church concretizes its historical will. The second fallacy is of a piece with the first. If the Church does not consider itself the progeny of natural causation, obviously it cannot see itself pressed to action by the urgency of temporal affairs alone. Lastly, when it acts it must, as a spiritual institution, seek to effect not only temporal gains, but eternal victories which are won, not in the arena of public affairs, but in the heart and mind of man.

These are the fundamental fallacies which bring the liberal hopes of Church cooperation to disillusion. Offsetting all theory is the anguishing fact that the Church, to the extent that it works in and through history, is as well a victim of history. The Church does not direct providence, but responds to it. As the individual both transcends and is victim of time and process, so the corporate individuality of the Church is likewise affected.

Assuredly it can be claimed that if papal excommunication would have stayed the hand of one murderer in the past three decades it would have been justified to excommunicate. There is indeed the Rabbinic dictum: "He who saves the life of one human being is accounted as though he had saved the whole world." But it is equally true that such excommunication, boldly enforced, might have weakened the spiritual mobility and effectiveness of the Church in Catholic countries where papal discretion would have been strongly contested. In effect, though I do not resolve the issue by posing the dilemma, it is clear that the Church is not immune to the perplexities that beset those compelled to practical decisions. The Church is caught between two goods or two evils and is incapable of determining for which to decide. The moral law will, of course, decide with apodictic clarity; but only where the moral law is stated *in vacuo*. The moment the decision is defined, the moral law enters the lists of ambiguity and casuistry. The more perplexing the circumstances, the more complicated the factors, the more people involved, the more destinies at stake, the more impossible it becomes to decide. It is for this reason that the papacy has often chosen to be silent. It is frequently difficult or impossible to understand the decision of the Church—whether to speak or be silent—but it is eminently clear that, however she choose, the choice is not made in response to sheer power or authority.

It is equally naïve to imagine that the Church can, by power alone, transform the human heart. It is argued that had the Church not sided with the Carlists and landowners the issue of land redistribution (an issue catalytic to the Spanish tragedy of 1936) might have been resolved. The Church could have exercised its moral authority to compel the landowners, including itself, to give up enormous holdings to the people. Such authority might well have strengthened the moral position of the peasant, justified him in his complaint, and solidified his community; yet authority and power could not produce the love or fellow-feeling which would make such division of land amicable or peaceful. It might be argued that what is sought is not love, but simple justice; that love is too exalted an objective to be won through political power. The economy of power, it is argued (as it is now argued with respect to the issue of racial integration), demands that authority support justice and basic rights and let love and fellowship come in their own time. Such a position can be justified by the state (which is at best only power in support of prevalent values), but it cannot be justified by a religious order which demands more than simple justice. The Church in Spain is indubitably reactionary, but such admission does not alter the fact that the papacy, when it decides to speak in the political order, must seek not only the efficacy of power, but the formation of a more profound and lasting human community. Were it to speak merely out of strength, it would succumb to the historical process, rather than seeking continually to transform that process into something which serves humanity more profoundly.

For the natural Jew power is an instrument of justice. He can only conceive of the utility of power in the service of immanent justice. Having secularized the position of the prophets, he must empower what the prophets drained of power; he must render to authority, to the state, to society, precisely the power which vanishes before the spirit of God. Where Jeremiah will despise the relevancy of power the natural Jew will enthrone it in the service of justice, charity, liberalism, and progress. He will respect power, it is true, but he will conceive its proper employment to be in the cause of just ends. The secular Jew will bring to the world a passion for justice which is but the obverse of his memory of disaster. He will balm the world in retribution for the pain it has rendered to him. The historical memory of the Jewish people is the impetus to the concern for justice which animates the natural Jew.[2]

## II. The Supernatural Jew and the Theological Image of the Church

It is well known that Pius XI, in a discourse offered before the directors of the Belgian Catholic Radio Agency in September, 1938, commented upon the words of the Canon of the Mass,

2. One is appalled that Joseph Bonsirven, S.J., an otherwise judicious and sympathetic student of Rabbinic tradition, so misconceives the character of the natural Jew. Indeed, in his pamphlet for the Catholic Truth Society, *Modern Judaism*, he repeats the conventional jargon of racial anti-Semitism. "As for the irreligious Jews, it may be that they no more respect the moral law than they do the religious law: and it is from their ranks that are recruited the men of shady business, the procurers of vice, and the instigators of social disorders." Can it be that Father Bonsirven suggests that religiosity is a sufficient evidence of virtue, that only the irreligious spawn vice and disorder? One might recall to his memory countless prelates whose natural virtue was, to say the least, noticeably defective. Indeed the distinction between natural and supernatural, as the distinction between irreligious and religious, is more subtle. The natural man, that is, he who does not acknowledge the mandates of revelation and the bequests of grace, may—and often is—a more profound servant of the Kingdom of God than many—far too many to please me—religious. Cf. *Modern Judaism*, Catholic Truth Society, London, 1954, p. 20.

*sacrificium Patriarchae nostri Abrahae.* "Notice," Pius XI said, "that Abraham is called our Patriarch, our ancestor. Anti-Semitism is incompatible with the thought and sublime reality expressed in this text. It is a movement in which we Christians can have no part whatsoever. . . . Anti-Semitism is unacceptable. Spiritually we are Semites."

This statement of Pius XI has become the stand-by of Catholic apologetes and theologians. It is obviously so important in the eyes of Catholics as to create an imposing effect by mere utterance. Nevertheless, it is not quite clear to me what the phrase means: is it pious rhetoric or does it, in truth, announce some profundity which had been obscured in the life of the Church? In all charity, one should grant that it is both a piety and a profundity. Any pontifical statement in 1938 was, at best, able to register a piety; it was, alas, too late for the papacy to effect any substantial penetration of the German conscience. As a profundity, his observation survives the occasion of its deliverance. Hitler is gone and six million Jews are dead. The piety is recorded, but the message survives.

Anti-Semitism is, as Léon Bloy observed in *Le Vieux de la Montagne*, a slander against "the Jew of Jews by nature."[3] This fact is recorded in the history of Christian faith. It is a moving fact, but is it more than a fact, one more fact within an order of facts? Clearly the fact that Jesus of Nazareth was a Jew can have, for the Jew, little more than irenic significance. It can be significant, moreover, only to those Catholics who choose to recall that the family of Jesus is a Jewish family. But this is only to recall the Catholic to charity before nature. Ancestral piety such as this may forestall some new outbreak of anti-Semitism; it may have served Léon Bloy in his reproof of the Assumptionist Fathers

3. *Pilgrim of the Absolute*, Pantheon, New York, 1947, p. 267.

and Drumont. It can little avail, however, before the supernatural destiny of the Jews. Semitic spirituality can be little more than a device of Catholic self-illumination for the reason that the House of Israel, the Jewish people, affirm a supernatural, not a natural, relation to the Christian world. What is fact to the Christian is irrelevancy to the Jew, for the reason that salvation according to Jesus Christ is, for the Jew, "ex Judaeis" but not "pro Judaeis." The Christian is saved out of Israel, but Israel is not saved and its redeemer is not come. The utterance of Pius XI can mean something only to the Christian. It can confirm a retrospective dependence and loyalty; but from the viewpoint of Israel which looks forward to The Coming such common links have validity only within the order of nature and history. The mystery of Jewish unbelief which confounds Christendom is from the side of Israel the mystery of trust.

To be related to the Jew, as Abraham is related to the world of Semites, supplies the Christian with, at best, a tenuous relation. The Jew does not recall out of Scripture a Semitic past, but a past fashioned in the devisings of providence. Indeed it is instructive to observe that, not Moses, but Abraham—the father of faith—locates the Semitic lineage of Christianity. Abraham, the first but not sufficient patriarch of Israel, has become the precursor of Christianity. Through an essentially analogical rendering of the narrative of Abraham, a pilgrim of grace is created to contrast with the reign of the Law. Abraham becomes the anticipation of Jesus. It is not for the Jew to condemn an analogical reading of Scripture; rabbinic tradition also exhibits a penchant for analogy and paradigm which exceeds the strict evidence of the text. The only reason for quarreling with the theories of modern spiritual archaeologists is that they take a form which cannot fail to put off the Jew. The fact that the very concept of the "Semite" is eighteenth century in coinage; that the term initially was intended to describe rather cavalierly a configuration of languages;

that the term came, by the late nineteenth century, to signify a *race* with very conspicuous physical, psychological, and social eccentricities belies for the Jew the high spiritual intention of "Semitic spirituality." If the lineage from Abraham to Moses and the Prophets is deemed Semitic, then either an imprecise term is employed or a racialism, foreign to both Jew and Catholic, has been elevated to transmit some ultimate reality to which it is essentially unequal.[4]

One cannot but feel, in sum, that the proclamation that "Spiritually we are Semites" rests upon a fundamental error. The statement would have been more correct had Pius XI said: "Spiritually we are Jews." The term "Semite" is a racial locution which cannot even be justified in 1938 as papal irony. To have said that Catholics are spiritually Jews would have been, however, a half truth for both Catholics and Jews. The truth is more complicated and mysterious. An erroneous statement of papal solicitude has, in effect, done little more than to confuse thought further by having first confused language.

## III. "The Mystery of Israel"

The condescension of Christianity toward the House of Israel and the faith of the Jews, perhaps more than all else, is deeply offensive. It is an offense which, to be sure, can be theologically rationalized. Whether Israel is conceived of as arrested child or aged father matters little, for the image of solicitude marks the attitude of the modern Church.[5] The Church no longer looks upon the Jew with astonishment and lack of comprehension. The

4. Cf. S. D. Goitein, *Jews and Arabs*, Schocken, New York, 1955, p. 19, for a pentrating discussion of the meaning of the term "Semite."
5. This is no less the stylistic hallmark of the declaration on the Jews of the recently concluded Vatican Council.

Jew is no longer, as he was until the waning of the Counter Reformation, a species of devil, a partner of heresy and iniquity. He is less than these—he is adjudged to be the victim of insufficient love. The Church—in some massive reversal of attitude, a penance, if you will—exhibits its contrition by love. Surely the Church should love. We would not gainsay the works of love. And yet love which is indifferent to strategies and unresponsive to effects is more convincing than the transparently calculated devices of formal love symposia. Though the attitude of the Church toward the House of Israel has changed from dismay to solicitude, the Jew is still the *object* of an action—a mere object. The Jew still plays a formal role in the masque of Catholic thought. The choreography is less frantic, but the love is still choreographed.

It is perhaps an unavoidable consequence of Catholic thought that the Jew is necessary to the fulfillment of Christian eschatology—that whether one preaches at him or simply loves him, the end is the same: to convert him. It may be unavoidable, but surely a heavy price is paid for keeping ends so clearly in mind. The price in this case is that the love is untrustworthy, a façade, a device. Once hate and now love—it matters little (other than in the economy of survival) whether we are slain outright or slain by condescension. In either case what is compromised is most essential, viz., that Israel be conceived not as an object of salvation, but as its agent.

The objectification of love is never more apparent than in the revival of the Pauline conception of "the mystery of Israel."

> What then shall we say? That the Gentiles who followed not after justice have attained to justice, even the justice that is of faith. But Israel, by following after the law of justice, is not come unto the law of justice. Why so? Because they sought it not by faith, but as it were of works. (Rom. ix, 30-32.) I say then: Hath God cast away his people? God forbid! (Rom. xi, 1.) I say then: Have they so stumbled, that they should

fall? God forbid! But by their offense salvation is come to the Gentiles, that they may be emulous of them. Now if the offense of them be the riches of the world and the diminution of them the riches of the Gentiles: how much more the fulness of them? . . . For if the loss of them be the reconciliation of the world, what shall the receiving of them be, but life from the dead? For if the firstfruit be holy, so also is the lump: and if the root be holy, so are the branches. And if some of the branches be broken and thou, being a wild olive, art ingrafted in them and art made partaker of the root and of the fatness of the olive tree: boast not against the branches. But if thou boast, thou bearest not the root: but the root thee. Thou wilt say then: The branches were broken off that I might be grafted in. Well: because of unbelief they were broken off. But thou standest by faith. Be not highminded, but fear. For if God hath not spared the natural branches, fear lest perhaps also he spare not thee. See then the goodness and the severity of God: towards them indeed that are fallen, the severity; but towards thee, the goodness of God, if thou abide in goodness. Otherwise thou also shalt be cut off. And they also, if they abide not still in unbelief, shall be grafted in: for God is able to graft them in again. For if thou wert cut out of the wild olive tree, which is natural to thee; and, contrary to nature, wert grafted into the good olive tree: how much more shall they that are the natural branches be grafted into their own olive tree? For I would not have you ignorant, brethren, of this mystery . . . that blindness in part has happened in Israel, until the fulness of the Gentiles should come in. . . . when I shall take away their sins. As concerning the gospel, indeed, they are enemies for your sake: but as touching the election, they are most dear for the sake of the fathers. For the gifts and the calling of God are without repentance. For as you also in times past did not believe God, but now have obtained mercy, through their unbelief: so these also now have not believed, for your mercy, that they also may obtain mercy. For God hath concluded all in unbelief, that he may have mercy on all. (Rom. xi, 11-32.)

St. Paul characteristically commences each address to the nations with reminiscence of the history and condition of Israel. Israel and the Gentiles form the continuum of dialectic: that wherein Israel has fallen is the occasion of salvation for the Gentiles; the rejection by which Israel is cast off becomes the opening of salvation to the nations. Presumably, without the action of God, Israel would not have fallen. Were it not for the determination of God, which confirms Israel in its rejection of the Gospel, the nations would not be availed of salvation. Israel is an enemy for the sake of the nations; Israel is beloved of the nations for the sake of that which makes possible, in the order of providence, the giving of salvation. But then it would seem God is the instrument of the unbelief of Israel: He confirms the alienation of Israel that He might avail the Gentiles of grace. Is this more than the effort of the Apostle to theologize a fact: That Israel rejected Jesus as Christ and remained faithful to the Law? Earlier he observed that the Gentiles sought "the justice that is of faith" whereas Israel, seeking, not justice as such, but "the law of justice," was disarmed by the announcement of the sufficiency of faith. But does not St. Paul define his antinomy by an inversion of language? For whereas the nations seek justice—and discover justice by faith —the Jews seek "the law of justice"—which, if law alone, perforce casts out the sufficiency of faith. Paul seems to gain his point by a deception of language, for the Jew does not seek the law of justice, but only the just law. No Jew—surely not the rabbis of the Christian Era—imagined that the Law, as such, was sufficient if it was not also the law "of the Lord"—that is the law conditional before the will of God. The law was not the end of salvation, but its means. As means, law was also conditional to faith—not in the law but in the Creator of Law, the Holy One, Blessed be He! Is such a law to be contrasted with faith? Are works to be juxtaposed to faith and law confounded when the face of faith is illumined? Surely not! Such a juxtaposition is a fiction to the House of Israel. Having called faith to the service of Jesus Christ and observed the rejection of Jesus Christ among the Jews, is it unreasonable that against Jesus Christ should come the law, and against faith the spurious sufficiency of good works? The theology of St. Paul, profound as it is, can be to the Jew but the impassioned effort to find reason for what seemed beyond reason. Indeed, given the faith of Paul, the recalcitrance of the Jew could not but be marked by some ineluctable bondage to law. Yet, given the admission of bondage (were it so!), Paul must, of needs, retain Israel that it be restored.

The mystery of Israel is, then, a mystery which is observed from the outside. It is a mystery which arises from the necessity of retaining what God so evidently sustains, of accounting for that people which denies and yet persists, which does not vanish in the smoke of unbelief, but endures in rejection and openness of trust before God. The mystery is, moreover, a datum of faith: for the partial shall be made whole, the incomplete shall be completed. Israel is somehow sustained, says Paul, until the Church has completed the task of redeeming the nations—then God cleanses Israel of sin (presumably the double sin of belief in the law and unbelief in Jesus the Christ), and brings her to the fullness of faith.

The faith of Paul in the last days of redemption and the introduction of Israel into the order of universal salvation is, from my understanding of the view of Israel, acceptable. Indeed, when the Messiah appears, the last days shall unfold before us and the universal order of salvation shall be inaugurated. Indeed (and such it may be), the redemption of those who were without God may, of necessity, be consummated endless years before the redemption of those who were called to God from their infancy. This is but to say that the Messiah who comes for Israel may be the same as

He who returns for the nations. But then it should be recalled that this is the action of God and the work of His grace, before which both Israel and the nations stand. Is it the work of the Church? We might grant that it is the work of the eternal Church, as, indeed, it is the work of the eternal Israel, to bring about salvation—the reintegration of Jew and Christian into the community of salvation. But is it the work of the terrestrial and visible Church? It is here that, as Jew, I must part completely from St. Paul. It is here that the Jew takes leave of those who scan the universe for mysteries.

For what is the "mystery of Israel" into which Léon Bloy and Jacques Maritain wish to induct both Jew and Christian? Maritain has said, "Israel is a mystery. Of the same order as the mystery of the world or the mystery of the Church. Like them, it lies at the heart of the Redemption." This is satisfactory. The way of the world, of the Church and of Israel is left open before God. Each has its structure, each its inheritance and its expectation, each presumably has its task. The convergence of task, the adequation of inheritance to expectation, the identification of structure, awaits a fullness of time and history in which God transforms world, Church and Israel. But M. Maritain is not satisfied with the parity of task: it is not enough to affirm that both Israel and Church pass through the ether of eternity and the substance of world together. More must be said and it is this *more* which sunders the community of Jew and Christian, Israel and Church. The Jews "chose the world; they have loved it; their penalty is to be held captive by their choice";[6] "the mystical body of Israel is an unfaithful and a repudiated Church."[7]

What is this but to say that, however their common sharing in

6. Jacques Maritain, *Redeeming the Time*, Geoffrey Bles, London, 1943, p. 133.
7. *Ibid.*, p. 134.

the "heart of redemption," there is a lower and a higher, a temporal and an eternal, a limited and an unlimited? Having projected Israel into the order of Christianity, Israel is assimilated to the theodicy of Christianity, and Judaism becomes a moment, a stage, an incompletion in the unfolding of Christian salvation. It is here that, for the Jew, the Christian faith becomes arrogant: assuming more truth than is consequential to its rightful possession of truth, more wisdom than follows from its true wisdom. For here Maritain (and to my mind Bloy[8] is an exaggeration, often an exceedingly vicious exaggeration, of Maritain's point) draws conclusions which neither Jesus Christ nor St. Paul would have commended. It is here that M. Maritain, like St. Augustine, believes because the witness of "the Catholic Church induces me."[9]

The inadequacy of Judaism is not established by the Pauline mission to the Gentiles. To the Jew, all of Pauline theology is a dialogue with the Gentiles in which the Jew is assumed and is silent. The dialogue functions, the theology is formed, the Gen-

---

8. I had been led to imagine that Léon Bloy's *Le Salut par les Juifs* was a transcendentally charitable work. I was mistaken. Indeed, the genius of Bloy lies in having polarized much more sharply, strenuously and uncharitably than Maritain precisely the points which I bring against Maritain. Surely Bloy is filled with solicitude for the Jew, but what Jew? Not the Jew who is confirmed in unbelief, who walks with God in the fullness of belief which is, for the Christian, unbelief. Bloy has solicitude for the Jew because he is outside the Church (and outside he is materialistic, corrupt, and dangerous) whereas he could be brought into the Church if he were loved. Now this is surely profound instruction for Christians, but it is for the Jew a distasteful and meaningless theologizing. Somehow, and I write this with a sense of exhaustion, Jews are tired of being used by Christians as the excuse for theology and then being rebuked for not believing the way such theology convincingly "proves" they ought to believe.

9. Cf. *epist. Manichaei ep.* 5. "Ego vero evangelio non crederem, nisi ecclesiae catholicae me commoveret auctoritas."

tile is converted—and all because the Gentile, not the Jew, is addressed. By contrast to the nations—who must still come to God and for whom Jesus Christ is the just and rightful medium—the Jew is obviously mysterious. After the Church has been formed and established—the converted pagan (who has been brought to God) or the converted Jew (who forgot that he might remember) addresses the Jew. But can they, indeed, address with such accents of certainty him who is with God by covenant and unrepented gift? Can the pagan address the Jew as "an unfaithful and a repudiated Church"? Can he who has won certainty by that which is compromise to the Jew—by a "God-man"—be sure that the Jew is not also with God and redeemed by God? The Jew does not confront the Gentile with the slander of his compromise, does not rebuke the Christian with having recourse to mediacies of incarnation and redemptive sacrifices; surely the Jew knows well what it is to be "suffering servant," to be ransom for the world in his own body and flesh and spirit without the vicarious atonement of *one* who ransoms *all*. The Jew does not condescend to the Christian by calling his faith "a mystery"—when all he might mean by mystery is that the Christian must come to God by scandalous means. And yet what does M. Maritain mean by the mystery of Israel other than the affirmation that a supernatural people has rejected "the means" of fulfilling its supernatural destiny?

In essence our repudiation of the concept of "the mystery of Israel" is not a repudiation of her mystery as such, but a repudiation of the Christian insistence that that mystery has value, truth and ultimacy only in so far as it is an aspect of the mystery of the Church. The Jew is unconcerned with contingent mysteries, mysteries which are dependent upon revelations other than the one revelation of which the Jew can properly know: that revelation which is the possession of the Torah and tradition.

## IV. Jewish Pelagianism

It is only natural, having established the polarity of action and grace, works and faith, law and Jesus Christ, that Christianity should come to see in Judaism a species of enduring Pelagianism. This would strike one as odd were it not for the fact that the language of Christian critics of Judaism abounds with expressions which are identical with those which St. Augustine leveled against Pelagius.[10] Pelagius is reported by Caelestius, his disciple, to have believed that the sin of Adam did not corrupt all mankind; that the Law, as well as the Gospel, leads to the Kingdom; that everything good and everything evil is done by man and not born with man; that the *posse* of man is uncorrupted, for it is a gift of God, but that sin derives from man's *velle* (violition) and *esse* (existence). It would follow that a tradition which rejects the offer of salvation, which refuses incarnate grace and the gifts which are contingent to that grace, is either vain or foolish in its estimate of human capacity. The Jew becomes Pelagian by failing to be Christian. His Pelagianism is a consequence of his being in sufferance to Law rather than grace. Lacking a doctrine of grace Judaism must, it appears, have an improper conception of the capacity of will, the possibilities of freedom, the ability of man. The Jew is Pelagian since the world, according to his lights, has neither properly fallen nor been properly redeemed.

10. The recognition that Catholics convict Judaism of Pelagianism first became clear to me in a review of my book, *Martin Buber*, which William F. Lynch, S.J., wrote for *America* (March 22, 1958). On that occasion Father Lynch observed that what I had described as the Christian criticism of Buber's "activism" was perhaps nothing more than the criticism of his Pelagianism. This is an obvious *petitio principi*.

I should be the first to admit that there is truth in the criticism. Construed most generously, Pelagianism embraces—as does the employment of all language of heresy—more errors than it properly signifies. If Pelagianism means theological optimism, shallow conviction about the unfolding of progress and order, there is much in modern Jewish thought which is annoyingly Pelagian. Such Jewish Pelagians are, by and large, naturalists—for whom little more than optimism could yield their bright and hopeful union of reason and the cosmos. Jewish Pelagianism is Jewish *faute de mieux*: it can be taken seriously as a Jewish ideology— a symptom of religious embarrassment—not as Jewish theology. Presumably the concept of Pelagianism cuts deeper than a merely ideological divergence, for what is meant is that Judaism is essentially Pelagian.

What are the marks of Pelagianism? insistence upon the capacity of man to fulfill the will of God; a judgment upon the sufficiency of man's will and freedom; a hopeful estimation of the possibility of human nature before God. The Pelagian commences by affirming that man is not condemned from the beginning; that, if he be condemned, it is through his own works that condemnation is wrought; that, if he be redeemed, it is through his contrition and penance that the occasion of God's redemption is supplied.

Clearly Pelagianism is not a dead heresy within the Church; nor, for that matter, is Marcionism banished. Great heresies do not perish nor do they pass away: they function as checks and guards against imbalance, they surround sound doctrine as an avenging angel stands at the precincts of the Garden of Eden to prevent the return of the old Adam. Great heresies warn us of their approach and caution us against their power. When the Church was tempted by Marcionism, Pelagianism came conveniently to caution it. Both were heresies, but together a truth was fashioned: creation was neither abandoned nor empowered.

All was left to God. This truth was appropriate to the Church, for indeed one could not in fealty to the Son, the Redeemer, abandon the Father, the Creator; nor in testimony to God, the Creator, could one compromise the redemption which was through God the Son.

Sound doctrine as this might be to Christians, it is unavailing to Jews. The heresies of Christians are not heresies to Jews, nor are the heresies of Israel the heresies of the Church.

Judaism suffers from an incapacity for a Christian vocation. It is not irony, however, which invests such an obvious assertion with portent. The polarities of law and grace which permit the imputation of Pelagianism to be seriously countenanced depend upon differing conceptions of the relation between the natural and the supernatural. The strength of the Church seems to me to lie in her single-mindedness: ability to lead souls to salvation by drawing around herself a line which separates the world from the Kingdom of God. The strength of Israel is her insistence that God leads creation, without cessation or condemnation, to redemption; that we are bound to creation in a work of coredemption which undergoes no transfiguration until the end. Where Maritain will write that Israel's destiny is both ennobled and limited by its unrelenting activism in the temporal order,[11] Israel will reply that the vocation of Christianity is often a betrayal of the temporal order.

The Pelagianism of the Jew consists in the fact that Judaism does not acknowledge the advent of the Messiah. This is an inescapable conclusion. But the price of this unbelief is no simple naïveté. Judaism is not naïve about the nature of man. It is perhaps more unrelentlingly realistic than its theology might suggest. But this is as it should be. Theology should direct but never regulate life—keeping open the possibilities of trust before God,

11. "The Mystery of Israel," p. 136.

maintaining contact with those resources of which only God can avail. For the Jew to abase himself before God, to renounce will, to abjure the essential divinity of the created order would be to commit suicide. Being unredeemed, the Jew cannot repudiate that which brings the universe to redemption; being unsaved, he cannot deny the only medium through which he joins with God in the performance of their tasks. Creation is the supernatural origin of history. History must be kept open if it is one day to rejoin and complete creation.

Jesus Christ is, from the Jewish point of view, no guide to the world, because the Christ vanquishes the world before its time. "I have overcome the world." In this sense, the anarchism of the *Philokalia*, Father Zossima, and Dorothy Day are of a piece. History—"the world"—exists only to be rejected, for it no longer conditions the life of the saved. The saved enter a different order of time and history in which to await—before the face of the world —their final turning from it. The evident fact that history *does* exist, that *holy history* touches and enters its flow, but does not overcome it, is, for the Jew, evidence of a high order that history is not yet marked with the transforming power of the divine.

The only principle which the Jew can use to judge history is one which asserts that history is turned toward the end, that it is open before God, that it awaits His grace, that it posits faith without end and without object, that, in short, it trusts God to fulfill and justify our love and sanctification of Him and His creation. This trust is Pelagian because it insists upon continuing the struggle when the witness of Christianity would have us already saved. It is deeply pessimistic and un-Pelagian because, unlike Christianity, it continues to insist that history be unsettled, that the idolatries and sureties of the world be probed, that false hope be smashed, that deceiving apocalypticism be chastened, that false and misleading redeemers be denied.

We are not Pelagians precisely because we deny that Jesus is the Christ. Indeed the case could be argued differently. It might be said, "Pelagian Jew, you have such trust in your law and in your works, you hope for so much from this world, that you ignore its real corruption, its real incapacity, its real defection. In Jesus the Christ you are given proof of God's mercy, that he judges the world so corrupt and in bondage to sin that he must give of himself that you be saved. Oh, foolish and stubborn Pelagian Jew!" We should reply: "Christian! How do you conceive God that you would have him imprison all men in disobedience that he might have mercy on all? Is this the same God, who once repented of the flood and promised never again to destroy creation? Is it he who gives us over to bondage that we should be freed? The contrary is the case, for God has given in his Torah an order for the universe which if we but follow and, through it, sanctify creation, then creation will find favor, and redemption will come to praise it—not rescue it—for all eternity."

The difference lies then in the valuation we place not on potency but on actuality, not on the possibility of working perfection but on the indescribable actuality of creation. Where Christianity would rescue us from corruption, Judaism would bend us to sanctification. Both movements of the spirit—that which would redeem and that which would sanctify—may ultimately be joined. The rescued and the sanctified—he who is ransomed by faith and he who struggles in the law—will both find their way to God.

## V.  The Untold Mystery

It cannot be hoped that Christian and Jew may find their way to conversation by mere self-exposure. It is not only that the Jew is ignorant of Christianity—locked in that invincibility of ignorance by which Christianity interprets its failure to convert the world—or that Christianity is ignorant of Judaism—satisfied as it is by an exclusivism which even the assertion of truth and universality fails to mitigate. Judaism and Christianity are different, utterly different. It is only the illusion of a temporizing equalitarian society which imagines that the Judeo-Christian tradition is a reality. It matters little that both traditions draw upon a common past, a common providence, that both make appeal to the same God. Such community serves only to accentuate their difference, for if such community were profound (if it were not merely the defensive truce which a pervasive secularism has enforced), the cliché and barren slogan in which it finds articulation would have vanished. We would have ceased to converse in the resounding strophes of the politician—who knows that all is difference but must insist that differences are minor and private. I do not believe that the difference between Judaism and Christianity is minor, nor do I imagine that the difference is one of mere accent and private idiosyncrasy. The myth (and I do believe that it is a myth) of the Judeo-Christian tradition obscures the vast chasm of being which separates the two faiths.

Christianity affirms a revelation by which the world of the dead and the world of the living are marked off forever, by which pagan and Christian, the damned and the saved, are separated as though by a lightning-bolt which cleaves the universe. Judaism affirms a revelation in Torah which has set forth the potency of creation; which regulates man in the actualization of creation; which directs man through history (which is but creation transposed from the vertical plane of *eternity-time* to the horizontal plane of *beginning-end*) to redemption. Christianity offers in Jesus Christ the promise and certainty of life. Judaism offers the world not the certainty but the choice of life, believing that only by choice (man's inordinately Pelagian choice) is creation authentically sanctified. We are divided by our truths, and our truths project vastly different conceptions of the essence of life and the human task and end. Where St. Paul might argue that the Jew imagines that law will yield perfection, that by the Law man might be delivered from sin—and despairs because the Law of itself is insufficient to afford such deliverance—he seems to forget what for the Jew is so obvious. The Law does not justify, but God justifies the Law. When I, inadequate and insufficient Jew that I am, accept the Law, do I imagine that sheer performance spares me of judgment, that the Law of itself gives salvation? Surely not! I must, always and everywhere, address myself to heaven and give over my soul to God that he judge me. The Law is but my "shield and my buckler," the viaticum of my life's passage, my provision against anarchy and chaos. It is a sea wall against time and history, not an assurance of eternity and the kingdom of God. It is, as are all things of faith, a risk.

Given the chasm of being which separates the two traditions, one certain that faith is capable of transcending the afflictions of the world and giving peace and the other committed to the afflictions of the world and the pursuit of peace, how can there be communication between them? The Church is dismayed by the unbelief of Israel. It formulates doctrine by which the authentic *corpus mysticum* of Israel is made doubly mysterious by its defection and default. Judaism is seen as but a conundrum in the life of the Church, a conundrum which God will resolve—in the meantime the Church maintains an attitude of spiritual *hauteur* and solicitous affection. Judaism, by contrast, can look upon the Church with inquisitive fascination: with its natural eyes it fears and suspects the power of the Church; with its supernatural eyes it validates the action of the Church in bringing the pagan to faith, but holds *itself* ultimately empowered to lead the pagan from the private precincts of faith into the anguished struggle for the Kingdom of God.

It is written in the classic commentaries of the rabbis: "Just as it is not possible for the world to exist without the winds, so it is not possible for the world to exist without Israel." As with all rabbinic exegesis, language is not chosen carelessly. The analogy of Israel to the winds is devised with precision. As the wind disturbs the composure of the landscape, raises the dust from the earth, explores the hidden places where there is darkness, so Israel is to the universe. It disturbs and dislocates the universe. The peculiar effect of Israel upon the world is not one that either Christian or Jew conceives to be the natural consequence of history and fate. Israel is a holy community, born out of the wedding of God and a peculiar people. Israel has always been a mystery to Israel. But it is a mystery on its own terms. This mystery has yet to unfold before the world. It is still untold what its mysterious presence in this universe may bring forth.

# The Encounter of Judaism
# and Christendom

THE DISCORD of religions is as often created from the default of mutuality as from the direct encounter of faiths. The relations of Judaism and Christianity have been singularly illustrative of this truth. In the past it was more easily possible for the Jew to withstand poignant encounter with the Christian experience. The contemporary development of a more comprehensive and sensitive Christian theological attitude vis-à-vis the Jew has rendered this inadequate. It is no longer possible to maintain that impeccable aloofness which it has been traditional for Judaism to display toward Christianity. The emergence of more subtle noncoercive modes of approach, illuminated most remarkably by Bloy, Berdyaev, and Maritain, has suggested the conditions of the dialogue.

The negation of Jesus as Christ by his Palestinian contemporaries was not a conscious or explicit phenomenon. The Gospels, *prima facie*, are not to be rejected in their historical account of Jesus' relation to the Jews. Much, however, that they record of the Jews' reaction and antagonism moves beyond the scope of narrative into the less accessible region of theological conviction. It is difficult to believe that many Jews knew of Jesus, much less formed an opinion of his works, or acclaimed the preposterous cruelty of his execution.[1] The history and its details are, however, of secondary importance. It is religiously pertinent that the Jew announce as an assertion of faith, not of history, that he has neither encountered, judged, nor denied the true Messiah.

The history of Christian overture, apologetics—and, in its bitterest moments, violence—compelled, however, where no encounter compelled, the Jews to the confrontation of Jesus as Christ. It was neither a confrontation of wish nor the compulsion of an inexorable destiny. It was rather the refraction of a potential mutuality that had never once found consummation. A possibility whereby to have decisively encountered and rejected Jesus Christ *was* offered. The life of Jesus, his Passion, his affirmed Resurrec-

1. Herford, *Christianity in Talmud and Midrash,* Williams & Norgate, 1903. It is Herford's thesis that wherever the Hebrew term *"min"* (sectary) or *"minuth"* (sectarianism) is employed in the Rabbinic or Talmudic literature, there is an explicit or veiled reference to Jesus, his ministry, or his following. In a literature of many hundreds of pages he has been able to locate only one hundred and thirty-nine passages suggesting such contexts. Of these a pathetically small number are indisputable in their allusions to Christianity.

The literature concerning the precise designation of the term *"min"* is extensive. There is at least considerable doubt that the term is primarily anti-Christian. I subscribe rather to the view first elaborated by Friedlander that the term suggests repudiation of the heresies of Gnosticism. Generally, however, the concept of heresy is never as specific in Rabbinic literature as it has subsequently become. It is used to condemn a variety of sins: metaphysical liberality, theological scepticism, moral iniquity, ritual laxity, inhumanity, et cetera. All are in receipt of the description "heretic." In this context it is, however, significant that where a reference to the life of Jesus occurs, the most basic details of his life are missing. It is not known specifically whether he was stoned or crucified. It is thought he was killed in Lydda, not Jerusalem. Such confusions indicate, however, that within a hundred years of his death, acquaintance with minimal details of his life had passed. It is difficult to imagine consequently that during his life his influence was as profound as the Gospels suggest.

tion gave ample basis to an experience. The presuppositions of experience, necessitating an experient as well as the objective reality, failed in this instance of fulfillment. It is a profound misconception therefore to speak of the rejection of Jesus. It is more bitter, but surely more accurate, to admit that Jesus was never known, never confronted, never met. He was never rejected by Israel.

The Jew, however, through his history of contact with Christendom, has come to fix an attitude which his ancestors never assumed. Post-Palestinian Judaism knew that a rejection of Jesus would have been at least intuitively justified. The rejection of Jesus was consummated in history, not in the *Kairos of* the Christ. What rejection there is, what inescapable contest and denial it has been the Jews' necessity to affirm, is the creation of time and not the working of the Eternal in time. This is not merely to admit that with the Christians' regrasping of that Eternal Moment, with the achieving of contemporaneity with the *Kairos,* and the true Imitatio Christi, the Jew will feel what he has, thus far, never felt. The Jew as Jew will never know Jesus as Christ. To accomplish such would be in fact to desist from his own reality.

It is not the Christian desire to convert the nominal Jew, the mere accident of birth. There is neither vindication nor glory in the receipt of a figment, an appearance. The contest is for the believing Jew, upon whom rests the yoke of the Kingdom. It is he whom the Christian seeks. It is he who in his nature, who by his affirmation, who through that in which he stands cannot be touched. The eternal in time, the God-man is not merely an affront to pure monotheism as is often thought. The problem does not center upon this theological doctrine. There is no metaphysics of monotheism in Scripture; it is the discovery of medieval Jewish philosophy (itself perhaps a contradiction in terms) that Israel possesses a rationally defensible truth. Nothing is farther from the experience of the pious.[2] His world is defined by the search for and encounter with God. It is a vivid, indissoluble, historical dialogue for which he stands. He cannot cease his relation with God at that Moment in history when it is asserted history is transformed, that the Dialogue is consummated, that the struggle for Redemption is over. His faith is born with the Beginning and is consummated at the End. There is between only the repeated, anguished, and arduous struggle to meet again, to encounter, to renew as of old. It is this historical dialogue which most profoundly distinguishes the Jew in belief from the assertion of Christianity. It is for this reason, and for no single issue of theology, that he feels himself most powerfully estranged from the Gospel.

It is not my purpose to justify this position. It is one I believe and out of which my own faith has grown. There is, however, a function which this view of Judaism may afford in contrast to the one traditionally held by the sympathetic of Christian thinkers. It may indicate that the passion of Israel is a lonely passion, one that knows more of the endurance of suffering than that of vicarious sharing. It learns its attitude from what it encounters. As Moses formed his view of the Egyptian only when he saw a slave of his people beaten, so the Jew of history learns of his world in the perception of the anguish he must bear. The Christian

---

2. It had been implied by Maimonides' formulation of the thirteen basic articles of the Jewish faith that one who did not subscribe could not henceforth be thought a Jew. Maimonides, however, did not understand adherence to be nominal; rather the Jew, in accepting, must of needs understand and reason his faith to unalterable intellectual foundations. This implication drew the vigorous and profound challenge of many of the most renowned and pious of European Rabbis, who argued that piety, the fulfillment of the commandments, works, and love transcend the adequacy of any theological or metaphysical assertion. They denied, in effect, that philosophic formulation could gain priority over the life of belief.

has given witness in the terms of history to that to which a historical faith, taking deeply the flow and rush of events, must react. Judaism cannot react to Jesus for in its history there is no comparable archetype, eternally perfect, yet human, of corruptible flesh, yet resurrected. There is no static mark to which Judaism points. The Jew knows no center in time. There is merely repeated reaching and encounter. He must view Christianity as Christianity is, for he has always viewed himself and God has viewed him as at each moment he is. Jacob was attacked, Moses was assaulted, he who profaned the Tabernacle with his touch was slain. At each moment God discloses his valuation of time, at every moment he proclaims, teaches, reproves, and has compassion. To one moment without change there is no recourse. As Israel knew a prefigured destiny before Sinai so it will know a fulfilled destiny after Sinai. Sinai structures, but does not fix. It legislated for time with the commandments of eternity. The Law is eternally the will of God, notwithstanding the innovations to be established by the Kingdom of God. It is useless, therefore, to contend that the Jew does not encounter Christ, but only sinning Christendom; that Christians are corruptible, but the Christ is unblemished. He can know no other reality than the history of the generations of man. As he judges himself forever repentant to the sins of immediacy, he must weigh the enormities of others in the terms of immediacy.

I have spoken thus far of the religious Jew for whom the encounter with Christendom is an encounter of sorrow. He knows of Christ, therefore, refracted through the image of Christendom. I have sought to indicate that this is the decisive reality for the Jew, that any other is meaningless to the Jewish spirit. The last decades have, however, seen an alteration of view. Whereas the persecutions of Hitler are unutterable in the magnitude of their depravity, we cannot cultivate their memory and live.

The development of the scientific understanding of Judaism within the past two centuries brought in its wake the attempt of scholars to reconstruct the relations of Judaism and Christianity, to elicit again from weary history what truth it still concealed. An extensive Jewish literature treating of Jesus, the Disciples, and Pauline Christianity matured and expanded. Judgments fell, however, into two neat, though by no means unforeseen, categories. The scholars of orthodox persuasion, after careful, though often questionable, analysis deemed the doctrine of Jesus and the Primitive Church to be in its grandeur a perpetuation of Judaism and in its innovation undesirable. More liberal, yet decisively Jewish, thinkers saw in Christianity a legitimacy of right, a truth; yet one limited, essentially circumscribed by, and therefore resoluble to, its Jewish constituents. With the exception of such figures as C. G. Montefiore there is no forthright sympathy, although there is praise of Jesus. Never, never, with the limited and somewhat ambiguous qualifications advanced by Buber and Rosenzweig, is the view that Christian theology has toward Jesus Christ deemed meaningful or demanding.

There are subtle and significant presuppositions for the reawakened Jewish interest in Christianity. The emancipation of the Jew and the relative decline of the temporal power of the Western churches relaxed pressure. Jewish apologetics could for the first time appear in enlightened circles. It took, however, an enlightened form. While Moses Mendelssohn, the most outstanding intellectual spokesman of early Jewish secularization, was seeking the sophistication of his faith and the imparting of manners to Judaism, the great spiritualist revival of Eastern European Hasidism was at its height. It was the Enlightenment which produced, not only the *Wissenschaft des Judentums* (Science of Judaism) of Leopold Zunz (1794–1886), but Reform Judaism. Both were compatible means of achieving "civilizing" ends. The air of enlightenment invigorated the *Leben-Jesu-Forschung* (research in the life of Jesus). The challenge of Christendom evoked no more than the passion of scholarship. Only when the faith that could encounter Christendom is sapped can the dispassion to examine arise. Whereas Orthodox Jews feel the weight of Christendom so deeply as to be incapable of uttering its founder's name, the enlightened have achieved such urbanity as to speak it with intimate familarity.

I have stated extremes, but not meaningless extremes. Between the exaggerations, the truth is lodged concealed. It is clear that this academic encounter of Judaism and Christianity is not of meaning to either faith. Each successfully ignores the reality of the other. It vindicated demanding claims to the whole of man with the armamentarium of evidence, dates, history, and archeology. It vindicates nothing. The enlightenment has created tolerance, but, if one may risk an ambiguity, a nonexistential tolerance, for the attitude of good will engendered was created by default, and not by passion. Nothing has been resolved. No encounter has taken place. Neither have Christians become Jews nor Jews become Christians in sufficient number to cause reflection. Scattered conversions do not make the meeting of faiths more than fortuitous. Direct, challenging meeting remains unknown.

I deeply seek the meeting of faith. I do not seek my conversion. I do, however, envision that profound encounter of the heart which is both vivifying to the spirit and witness to the re-creating presence of God in history. The meeting, to be a meeting, must be forthright and without reserve. It must be a meeting of the I and Thou. Each is capable of creating himself, of complementing his spiritual life, by witnessing the life of the spirit in another. It is not necessary to specify who shall say these eternal words first. Firstness and priority know no context when it is from one's being that a man speaks to another. There is spontaneity and meeting.

It is in this light that one must affirm the meeting to transpire. Christianity cannot reprove Israel with the rejection of the Christ. Judaism cannot deny Christianity for its defection from the Torah. To speak of denial is to ask the question of rightness to the spirit, of priority, and self-legitimation. It is clear that there is discord. It is clear that the unity of anguished presence and the repose of love are infinitely more desirable than fractious and destructive pride. The Christian cannot, therefore, say the meeting must take place only through the confrontation of the Christ. Not only with the confrontation of the Christ is the I and the Thou spoken. To confront the Torah is to fulfill the wholeness of this mutuality. Israel is no mystery, as Maritain affirms. It is a mystery only in the sense that a dilemma, a riddle, or an enigma is unsolved. To speak of the mystery of Israel is to shut off Israel from penetration. Israel is not to be solved. She is to be loved and only from encounter can love flow. Christendom is not to be the Other One, the hated, the rejected, but the loved. Love is never the work of theological fiat. To make mere professions of love is not to enter the conditions of mutuality and meeting.

When the meeting transpires—for only through meeting can the rejection of Jesus be understood for what it is, an ontic difference, not a mere negation—the Jew and Christian will exchange something more profound than doctrine, for they will find with all difference, a common life. Perhaps this reality is inconceivable. Perhaps doctrine, learned thought, theological necessity, the way of the ecclesia, forbid meeting. Perhaps it is all a fancy to be dispelled in the vindictiveness that it has been the lot of millennia to witness. If, indeed, it is, Christians shall have surely denied the Christ, and Jews will have failed in their struggle to encounter the One.

# II.  Polemics
and Disputations

# Three We Have Lost:
## The Problem of Conversion

COMPLEX TRADITIONS are, more likely than not, sensitive to challenge and criticism. It is not unusual, therefore, that Judaism has remained, by and large, indifferent to the problem of religious conversion, for the convert is a challenge. If he enters Judaism from the non-Jewish world, he suggests by his presence that we possess a truth sufficient to draw him from the community of his ancestors to ours; if he leaves Judaism, he suggests by his defection that we are in error, that our doctrine suffers from incompleteness, that it fails to meet some precious human need that he finds fulfilled elsewhere. In either case the decision of the convert disturbs complacency and commands responsibility.

This is an age of conversion—political, social, religious. The convert is among us, and we must confront him or else lose the rare opportunity of seeing ourselves from the outside, for, indeed, the Jew who leaves Judaism achieves a vantage point from which he can consider us, whether with sympathy or bitterness, and report his reflections. Such will be neither necessarily accurate nor fair, but his reflections will always serve to disconcert wanton pride.

The converts from Judaism whom I shall examine share in common a single conviction: Jesus the Christ is the Incarnate

95

God who suffered to redeem Israel and, with Israel, the world. The born Christian would not place particular emphasis upon Israel. The convert does. Invariably he sees his role as a Christian rendered unique by his ancestry. He is of that people to whom the Messiah is promised. He has asked himself: "Is it true or is it not true that Jesus of Nazareth is the Christ, that he has redeemed me, Israel, and history; but that I, by obduracy or stupidity or error, have ignored his presence, that I wait vainly for a coming that has come, for a redemption that is at hand, for a moment that is past and is yet eternally present?" Unlike the faithful community of Israel, he has answered affirmatively.

The question posed implicitly by the convert to Christianity is formidable. Israel is pressed to consider again and again the ultimate question: who is Messiah? If this question can be asked (and to do so one must presuppose seriousness), all controversial challenges must be acknowledged, all possibilities must be essayed. If this is, indeed, a question on which the redemption of Israel and all mankind depends, then the appearance of even the most patent fraud invites and receives seriousness. For what other reason do the Bible and Talmud make explicit the conditions under which prophecy is validated, if it is not for the reason that even the most patent fraud, using signs and wonders, inspires credulity in the trusting. Jesus of Nazareth is, therefore, a challenge to the Jews; for if he is Messiah, Israel shall have toiled in error. If he is not Messiah, then we must continue to wait, labor, and trust.

*I*

The converts to be considered are all writing converts. They have set down their past and explored the sources of their present.

They are all Roman Catholics. They are Karl Stern, John Friedman, and the late Israel Zolli. Their books vary. Some supply the verbal remnants of spiritual history, whereas others seek to lay open the consequences of their new-found position. Some are passive, seeking merely to explore the private appropriation of a truth; others seek to make one conscious of that truth. Some are modest, others pretentious. It is what attitude they assume toward Israel that is of value. The converts do not expect that books will soften the adamantine hardness of centuries, nor are they unwise enough to imagine that their words will be received without reply. One hopes to elicit from their writings some understanding of their spiritual history. We hope to learn from them so that we may better answer them and prevent others from repeating their error.

## II

*The Pillar of Fire*, by Karl Stern, is a remarkable book, and Karl Stern is a remarkable man. He cannot be discussed, nor for that matter can the others of whom I shall write, unless it be assumed that he is genuine, that his struggle to decide truly is reported without guile. He is truthful, and what he describes is truthful, though not necessarily true.

Karl Stern was born in a small town in Bavaria some half dozen years, I would surmise, before the First World War. Bavaria is Catholic Germany. His parents were merchants, Jews among few Jews, disinterested Jews among other disinterested Jews. They knew enough of Israel and her ways to serve God but little. Compensating but slightly for the atmosphere of spiritual void was Stern's grandfather who lived with the family, knew and observed the Law, but thought it fit only for the aged and dying, for the generation that was passing. He thought, though he was filled with knowledge and sentiment for things passing, that the claim of Israel ought not to interrupt the flood of modernity. Side by side with this weak rural Judaism was, as is usual in peasant communities, a vigorous Catholicism, a Catholicism that penetrated the seasons with the accents of its ancestry, an ancestry neither the Jews of Bavaria nor young Stern recognized as being Jewish in origin until the time was past. It was a Catholicism that might well impress, for it textured life; whereas the Judaism Stern saw in those formative days of youth was nonexistent.

Stern came to Munich in his early youth. He boarded with an Orthodox widow and her family who served God in joy and completeness, and attended synagogue regularly—not the liberal synagogue, but the congregation of Rabbi Ehrentreu, a figure Stern admired both for his imposing sanctity and for the wholeness of his witness. At the same moment in his life he witnessed, as only a youth might, the baffling chaos, the political turmoil, and the economic uncertainty that followed the collapse of Germany in 1918.

The postwar years saw the youth of Germany splintered by spiritual waywardness—youth groups, the *Wandervögel*, movements of romantic excess and abandon. The Jews followed suit, though with Jewish romanticism. Stern belonged to an organization called the Young Jewish Wanderers. It did not matter what you thought, what commitments, if any, you might hold. If you were Jewish you could wander with the Jews. At this point in his story Stern describes three remarkable persons who emerged from this atmosphere of tension and disorder: Erna, the Jewess who became a Communist; Friedel, who, though unimaginative and slow, nevertheless committed his life to work and to Zion and eventually coupled both desires by settling in Israel; and Rudi, who moved from austere piety and study to become one of the first leaders of the Mizrachi farm movement in Israel. Besides Rudi, Stern comments tersely, "I was the only other one who had turned to religion." Though the family of Rudi admired his conversion, the parents of Karl Stern did not. His pieties were indubitable, but filled with anguish. Who, not among the returned to Israel, has known the pain of prayer, the wearying words of Hebrew that become light only when the words have been savored for years, when the words have ceased to be obstacles placed by the long-skilled between the initiate and God? Stern knew this anguish. He was late to meals, for it takes time to pray the morning service carefully. He kept the dietary laws, which irritated his nonobserving family. Finally it was Uncle Julius, the man from the outer world, a traveler to Ceylon and India, who made his young belief a mockery. Uncle Julius described many faiths and many creeds, all pretending to truth and authority. Since all are equally true or false, why exert oneself? Stern did not. Here was perhaps his error, but he was like many people who cannot maintain constancy in the face of the assailing variety of the world.

The story expands at this point, and the subtle interstices are filled too quickly. Stern becomes a doctor, a psychiatrist. He recalls small incidents that are significant—the quiet faith of simple Christians, maids, workers, servants, who did not live in the grandeur of the world, but were not seduced by it either. Hitler came. The world of the psychiatric institute was penetrated by Hitler. The persecutions began. The institute was involved in the first efforts of Hitler's barbarity, the sterilization of the mentally ill. "The National Socialist Revolution . . . acted like an earthquake and flood because masses of Jews were, in spite of years of gathering clouds, psychologically and ideologically utterly unprepared."

Jewry was all the more rapidly devastated because it was so remarkably assimilated into national German life. Zionism became almost immediately a powerful answer, and its ranks swelled. No longer an ideology, but a means of practical solution, *Weltanschauung* became programme. Stern speaks with openness and humility at this point, for though he says this Zionism with its "non-committal appendix of 'Jewish culture' " left him unfulfilled, he acknowledges the tremendous suffering others endured in pursuing its objectives. He returned instead to the Orthodox Synagogue. He speaks with admiration of Franz Rosenzweig and Ernst Simon. He studied Midrash and the Prophets with commentaries. With this reawakened sense of the religious continuity of Israel preserved by Orthodoxy he began also to think about the meaning of Israel. He became convinced of the validity of two critical concepts: the absolute truth of revelation and the centrality of the Messiah in Judaism. He became convinced of the personal Messiah.

It was at this point, in 1933, that he makes the acquaintance of three people: a Protestant Japanese couple and a Catholic woman, all attached to the Psychiatric Institute. These people considered the Hebrew Bible to be their Bible, though they were not Jews. They, like the members of the early Church, were not followers of Marcion. They believed in a Messiah who had come. The awareness that what bound them to him was a common belief in a merciful and redeeming God was crystallized, Stern reports, by his purely accidental attendance at one of Cardinal Faulhaber's famous sermons, in which the distinguished prelate proclaimed the continuity of Israel and the Church. "It had a profound and irrevocable influence on me." Stern's description of this sermon is brief, emotional, and unsophisticated. Its influence was, however, apparently irrevocable.

From this point on, the intellectual argument projected back into time is summarized. Some twenty years elapse, but Karl Stern is today a Roman Catholic.

The intellectual argument centers about the elaboration of two points: in 1933, two parties, Stern argues, maintained the racial wall around the God of Sinai—the Nazis and the Jews. "Let there be no mistake. Jewish religion up to this day is based on the axiom that Revelation is a national affair and the Messiah to the Nations has not been here yet." "Do not be misled," Stern tells us, "by fine personal ethics, and disjunct declarations of the Hebrew Fathers, and noble Talmudic principles about universality, for such statements are to ancient Israel but the 'invisible Church.'" They are, in effect, accidental. "Jewish religion is racial exclusiveness. Mind you, it was racial exclusiveness in its noblest, most elevated form—in its metaphysical form . . . It was racism exactly opposed to that of the Nazis, but it was racism just the same. It was racism with the highest, divine justification—as long as its one basic premise was correct, namely, that the Anointed One was still to be expected." The second question is clear: was the one who came announcing himself to be Messiah the true Messiah?

It is of no moment to proceed through the balance of the argument, which is but an argument to the specific mediacy of the Catholic Church. This is relevant to his personal history, but not pressing to us. It is enough to center on these two points throughout and leave other issues to another time.

## III

Dr. John Friedman, a South African Jew become Catholic, fits more closely than does Karl Stern the classic image of the Jew victimized by self-reproof and chastisement. He leaves Israel with obvious defiance and hostility. The testimony of his rites of passage is filled with rancor and bitterness. It is frequently foolish.

Nevertheless, his book, *The Redemption of Israel*, is noteworthy for being a modern restatement of the implications of the Christian exegesis of the Hebrew Bible. It is a study in Scriptural parallelism, a distinctly Christological parallelism. The history of Israel, as preserved by Scripture, is taken as an analogical anticipation of the coming of Jesus; the fate of Israel thereafter is read as God's damnation of Israel. Thus the title, *The Redemption of Israel*, for Israel can be redeemed only if it is repentant. Jewish doctrine agrees. Repentance, however, in Friedman's reading, is the acknowledgement of Israel's error and the contrite recognition that Jesus is, in fact, Messiah.

Friedman's argument may be summarized briefly. There are three epochs in Israel's history: the Egyptian, the Babylonian, the universal. Each is characterized by sin, punishment, survival through unmerited grace, salvation through repentance, and restoration. The classic Jewish sin (and Friedman is right in this) occurs between Israel and God and consists in "a unilateral attempt to break the Sinaic contract." The bondage in Egypt Friedman interprets as punishment for the sin of idolatry. Similarly, the sin that causes the wrath of the Babylonian exile. Again this is not radically different from classic Hebrew exegesis, although the didactic compassion of God is seen by Israel as the inner meaning of punishment, rather than the sheer wrath Friedman feels constrained to proclaim.

The universal epoch consists of one sin and an eternal punishment: the rejection of Jesus of Nazareth and, by consequence, the rejection of God and his covenant. Friedman interprets this unwillingness to acknowledge the mission of Jesus as Israel's repudiation of its "responsibility of going out into the world and undertaking the burden of its sanctification." Peter and Paul assumed this burden. They are, therefore, the true remnant of Israel. Israel rejected the Kingdom of God. The Catholic Church chose,

Friedman tells us, the Kingdom of God and left to Caesar the world. This is a dubious interpretation of Catholic history, to say the least.

If Jesus of Nazareth had been merely a prophet, as Montefiore and other liberal Jewish thinkers seem prepared to admit, Friedman argues, the "punishment" which has befallen Israel for two millennia is without reason. It seems, therefore, that Jesus was more, that the rejection of Jesus was a rejection of God, that God has punished Israel ever since, that the fate of six million Jews is somehow but the measure of God's wrath. Friedman leaves us no choice but that between his compassion and God's.

Thus far the theological argument: Israel's idolatry, racial parochialism, narrowness of vision, all conspire to cause it to reject its "King." For this Israel is "slain all the day."

The element of captiousness and rancor in Friedman's statement emerges in his discussion of Israel's fate in the Exile. The Synagogue, he holds, is corrupt beyond imagining; Pharisaic Judaism is utterly sterile and moribund; the Jew is without personality, imagination, creativity. The Jew is derivative, second-rate, posturing, self-righteous, convinced of his goodness when he is evil, his wisdom when he is ignorant. For pages on end irritation and disgust are devised to pass as subtle analysis. It is at best higher anti-Semitism that we encounter here. It becomes clear, moreover, that Dr. Friedman knows nothing of Judaism or Jewish history. Those he quotes to represent the Jewish spirit are by and large its secondary spokesmen, frequently its least qualified spokesmen. It is, indeed, foolish to call on Israel Zangwill for Jewish theology.

I suspect that John Friedman began to reflect on Jewish literature after he had resolved to become a Catholic. What I fear is that his Judaism prior to the Church consisted exclusively of Jewish nationalism. Friedman might well have been the racialist he repudiates, the nationalist he scorns. It is pertinent to note that he seeks the redemption of Israel in what he terms "Catholic Zionism." He is wholly committed to the restoration of Zion, but a restoration that proceeds by way of the coronation of the spiritual king Israel denies. He stands with Hebrew language and culture, with the rebuilding of Zion. He has apparently solved to his own satisfaction what has come to be the dilemma of Zionism. What is the dilemma of Zionism? It is, in brief, the fulfillment of an ideology whose conception and program were rendered potent only by its incompletion. When Zionism was fulfilled, when Israel became a state, it became obvious that its ideology was valid only for the Diaspora, that it had no ultimate orientation in terms of which to interpret the destiny of those who would not go up to the land to live. Its ideology depended upon the physical removal to Zion of Jews from all corners of the earth. As Karl Stern notes, this was an effective appeal in the crisis; yet not ideology but survival was the triumphant motive. When there was neither the imminence of destruction nor the pressure of dislocation, Jews did not make *Aliyah*. The ideology failed to supply anything more. Zion disappeared into statehood. God had long since disappeared. John Friedman writes like many a disenchanted Zionist. He writes like one who had given his life to Zionism only to discover that it was a doctrine which offered nothing beyond a spatial salvation, for indeed Zionism depended upon the physical location of the Jew in one place, Eretz Yisrael. He had no access to the prehistory of Zionism, the Bible, the medieval literature, the classic savoring of the invisible as well as the visible Zion. He describes a serious impasse. He instructs Israel out of his anger and stupidity, for he shows forth the lines of his inner crisis, the inability to trust a religious culture which had in the modern age divested itself so completely of its spiritual mission.

## IV

The baptism of Israel Zolli, Chief Rabbi of the Jewish community of Rome, into the Roman Catholic Church occurred on February 13, 1945. *Before the Dawn* is Zolli's effort to recount his conversion. Whether Jews like him or not, he cannot be casually dismissed. Whatever his neuroses, derelictions, or incompetencies, he was the guardian of the intellectual and spiritual life of one of the most ancient of Jewish centers. When such a man leaves Israel and embraces Roman Catholicism, his defection cannot help but become a *cause célèbre*, and by that fact, most pressing of assessment.

There are two ways in which the autobiography might be approached. Zolli's life might be subjected to searching scrutiny in an effort to show that the seeming Jew was never an authentic Jew, that the pious scholar was always an apostate underneath. Zolli assists one in this task. To those who wish to make him disappear with the wand of psychoanalysis, he has provided sufficient incidents. His youth was spent, he reports, in meditations on the Hebrew and Christian Testaments, in emotional ecstasies engendered by reflections on a crucifix in a friend's home, in passionate dedication to admittedly Christian formulations of the problems of divine love and suffering. The second way is to accept the man, but to examine his testimony. To be sure, there is no evidence that Zolli's past was as subtly flavored with Christian sentiments as he would now have it. Inevitably he sees his past from the perspective of the present. He interprets it, remembering what he chooses, forgetting what is better forgotten. We must, however, accept his testimony. His past is the key to his biography, not to the truth or falsity of his interpretations. We can learn nothing about religious truth or falsity from his personality or character. Such things can be learned only from his meditations and reflections. It is in this manner that his book must be approached.

Zolli formulates his fundamental dilemma as follows: "The Law or the law of Love; love of the Law or the law of Love. And this was my solution: the frigidity of a law, of any law, is tempered only by the warm rays of love." It is obvious that Zolli is challenged by the classic Christian antinomy. He is won by the Christian answer to it. In his eyes the Talmud is an arid wasteland, fertile in but few places. In formalizing the spirit of the Bible and turning it into law Judaism has, in Zolli's opinion, destroyed the Bible. Only the Zohar and Hasidic literature restore to the Biblical text its passion and searching anguish. Zolli has resented, even though the resentment is ludicrously overstated, what many contemporary Jews resent: the routinization of the spiritual life, the turning of the spiritual life into practical maxims. It is not the Law *per se* that disturbs him, but the Law unmoved by passion and exaltation. He raises a legitimate problem. The Law as Law, uninformed by an immediate sense of its humanity and compassion, will have considerable difficulty in regaining its ancient primacy. If the Law is the divine routine, then it must be seen as expressing all of God, his love as well as his justice. If the Law is to be tempered by mercy, mercy must be forthcoming not only in the extraordinary breach of the Law, but must also pervade and instruct its routine fulfillment. Rabbi Akiba refused to pass death sentence on an offender under any circumstance: this is God's mercy for the extraordinary transgressor. What, however, of the ordinary transgressor? For centuries rationalist defenders of the Law, who by and large fixed its character and dominion, considered suspect those who concentrated on the recovery of the hidden passion, intention, and purpose of the Law. The mystics who were thus denounced surely sacrificed something of canonical literalness, yet were aware, as perhaps many legalists were not, that the authority for the Law was not only a tradition that stretches back to Sinai, but the person and will of the living God.

Zolli, had he lived, might have discovered that the Catholic Church has bred its own legalism, its own maze of purposes and cross-purposes, protocol and etiquette—all of which would seem quite irrelevant to the pursuit of salvation. It has, however, remained catholic. In opposing its heretics it sought to convert them and their passion to legitimate uses. When it failed, it sought to destroy them—witness the Albigensians, the Huguenots, the Hussites, the Protestants. "Catholic" Catholicism had limitations of generosity. Whatever their hostility to heretics, the Jews could not and would not resort to the sword. Zolli's praise of Catholic universality may represent a theological wish; it is, however, questionable history.

When Zolli turns by contrast to Israel, he wonders about *its* catholicity. He asks: Where is the law of Love to complement the love of Law? There is a partial answer to this question which his conversion suggests. Israel is elect, that is to say, unique. It seeks to preserve its uniqueness through centuries of direct attack and attrition. The Torah is its unique possession. The Gospel is the possession of Christendom. The polemic of Christendom has formed the opposition of Torah and Gospel as the opposition of Law and Love. This is a false opposition. If Judaism were merely the rule of Law, there would be no way to explain its survival once its hierarchy of courts and system of punishments had broken down. If Judaism were merely Law, then this Law could not exist without a system of sanctions to enforce it. If Christianity were merely love, a pure feeling, it could not survive twenty centuries without exhausting this feeling. Like perfume it would have aerated itself, been diffused, and disappeared. Israel survives, on the contrary, because it encounters God through the Law, comes to love him, learns his ways, explores his will, seeks him, as commanded, with all its heart and mind and strength. Christianity, for its part, has developed a formidable discipline, a ritual law to channel its spiritual passion. The student of Talmud has his counterpart in the student of canon law. The Catholic who is remiss in the performance of his religious obligations finds beyond all love a law of indignation, chastisement, rebuke, and damnation. Catholicism has reintroduced the God of judgment at precisely the point where Israel left off. It could do no other, but it can well beware of the pride of imagining it is right and others are wrong, when both are actuated by the same necessities.


## V

It is difficult to explore the reasons for the "obduracy" of Israel in the face of Christianity. Many foolish things have been said by both Jews and Christians about each other. By and large, folly results from having substituted the minor complaint for the major problem, from having seen the totality through a part, an accidental attribute, a vagary of history. Indeed, much discussion between Judaism and Christianity has been corrupted by needless historicism. Both Jews and Christians are guilty of having committed in the historical order what Whitehead has accurately termed "the fallacy of misplaced concretion." The serious issues are few, but decisive. It seems valuable, therefore, if the Jewish reaction to the convert is to be understood, that these issues be stated. What follows, therefore, is an effort to formulate a theological response of Israel to the convert.

Jews believe, if they are to remain Jews, that Jesus is not the

Messiah promised by Scripture. It is enough to affirm this. It may be asked, if not Jesus of Nazareth, who, then, is the Messiah and when will he come? This question cannot be answered. It is indispensable to the Jewish position that it remain unanswered.

History is only seen against its past. It is easy to challenge Israel, for what it denies others accept. Christians can recall the subtleties of doctrine which have come to define for them what has not been for us. To say that Jesus is not the Messiah is to say that history is not yet redeemed for us. Jesus may indeed redeem history for the Gentile, for to accept him is presumably to be transformed by him. This is the nature of faith. If one gives his life to God he is transformed or, in truth, he has not given his life. So with the Christian. What he gives, he receives. This is so, even if from the view of Israel he has given in error. Israel has not given, therefore it cannot yet receive. It may be asked, why have we not given? We do not give, for we await God's own instruction, in his own time and in a form coherent with our past and consistent with the future our past has shaped. We cannot but view the description of Jesus as a "stumbling-block" to the Jews as accurate, but needless, pejoration. It is pejoration to the Gentile, but not to the Jew, for Jesus is a stumbling-block, and our obduracy is accurately defined. We are obdurate and justifiably so.

If Israel is chosen, it is chosen for a unique task—to outlast the world and its solutions, to be borne up to the end of time as His alone, to make a peculiar pilgrimage in the world which consists of examining the complacencies of the world and noting that what is there renders the burden of life supportable, where in fact that burden is unbelievably difficult to bear. This is an aristocratic and painful mission, for though it speaks to all the world and lays claim to it, it does not seek to convert it, for its message is more painful and courageous than the world can suffer to accept. This is the task of Israel. It is not as the Rabbi of Prague said at the moment the coming of Sabbatai Zevi was announced. We do not say with him that "the world is not changed," therefore we do not believe. It is only partially this, for the transformation of the world is not only that the wolf and the lamb shall share bread together or that war shall cease from the world. This is the social image of salvation which is true enough as far as it goes. The change in the world that comes in the wake of the Messiah is not only social change, for social change assumes only the restructuring of relations, the reordering of patterns. Social change assumes that the ultimate structure of the world, its being, is essentially perfect, but that its accidental ordering is awry. God does not work social change. He does not attend diplomatic conferences and political conventions. He does not improve good will. He works on a universe, in which nature and man participate. Where such conspire to close Him out of the world, it is not social error. Society does not reject God. It is the individual who turns Him out of his life. It is a consequence of his abysmal limitation that a man should not be able to follow after God. A man may follow after his beloved, or seek after beauty, but to follow after God is a task of infinite difficulty. This is the inner weakness of man, the flaw that renders the marble block useless. This is a condition of the structure of our world. The world is not *reformed* by the Messiah. It is *transformed*. This will come to pass, Israel believes, only when the world wishes it so deeply that it cannot abide itself more a single moment. At that moment the Messiah may come. This moment of expectancy has not yet arrived. Israel cannot but say that he has not come. The Rabbis have taught us that I, and all of Israel, prevent him from coming. Of this there is no question. We are not blameless for his having delayed, but we cannot escape concluding that he has not come.

If indeed it is the mission of Israel to watch the world, to strain its complacencies, its satisfactions, to break its illusions, can Israel stay within itself, not seeking out others, confronting others, challenging the non-Jew to examine himself? Can it be the self-enclosed society it has been, the secret seed that will not flower before all? Israel—Stern, Friedman, and Zolli tell us—is a self-centered people that will not show itself, will not leave itself open to the world. They see our nationalism as opposed to universalism. This is an error on their part which results from not understanding the nature of that nationalism. When Moses called for eternal struggle against the Amalekites, the symbolic hypostasis of evil, he bound Israel to the world. When Joshua and his descendants struggled against the seven nations who occupied the Land of Israel, we became further bound to the world. Each time God took Israel out of Zion he informed us, in effect, that we had become too attached to our place, that we had become comforted in our security, eased by our plenty. In such moments we always forgot Him. Moses warned us that this might happen. He warned us that in the luxury of the Land we might forget the Lord God. Israel did as Moses had forewarned, and God drew it forth and cast it on the stage of history to instruct it again, to compel it to rediscover Him in adversity. Each drawing forth—each Egypt and Babylon—is a drawing forth for instruction. In meeting Egypt and Babylon we are told that our destiny, though national, is not fixed to place, that we must belong to God, and thereby to his world, wherever we are. Each time Israel failed to open itself to God, shutting out thereby its responsibility to all of creation, it moved deeper into itself. This is our great error, one which our history instructs us is error. For we were never intended to be for ourselves alone, to disengage ourselves from the world outside our own, to discourage the convert, to withdraw from the history of mankind. This is what Israel has often done, and we have deceived ourselves and him who chose us. For this reason, many, seeking our authentic universality and finding it disclaimed, have turned elsewhere.

It is not easy to accept the challenge of history. It is at least questionable if, on the strength of Biblical interpretation *per se,* it can be demonstrated that Israel is intended to be bound to the history of mankind. I am willing to grant that the Biblical interpretations which precede have perhaps been strained to my own concerns, and are, therefore, inaccurate, subjective, and perverse. It seems equally true, however, that if it is inauthentic Judaism to strive to be universal, to achieve that nexus with the world for which we are repeatedly asked, why, then, is so much modern Jewish apologetics turned in the direction of proving our universality from classic sources? Presumably we are anxious that our integral community with the non-Jewish world be appreciated. This can, it is true, be merely a gesture of higher, ideological assimilation; it can be (more profoundly) a statement of our re-awakened awareness that God and Israel do not converse in perpetual, private dialogue, speaking grand and profound thoughts to be transmitted on a closed circuit. It is my own conviction that the isolation with which we are charged has resulted from the loss of interest in the Messianic character of Jewish thought, whether Messiah be understood substantively (the person of the Messiah) or metaphorically (the world-historical significance of Torah).

## VI

Perhaps the most difficult portion of any religious response to the presence of the convert from Judaism is the assessment of its ultimate, individual consequence. Surely the apostate from Catholicism is not treated with pluralistic good grace. When one forsakes truth it cannot be expected that one view the apostate with indifference. It is even questionable whether charity is applicable. Compassion, pity, sympathy, a sense of anguish—all these are plausible, but the fact of sin, grievous sin, is not displaced. One may have sufficient gentleness to leave the ultimate verdict to heaven, though the terrestrial instruments of power shall have pronounced anathema. The fact remains that the convert has sinned. Obviously it is not a moral sin, unless the convert forsake the truth to gratify lust or passion for power and security. Even then moral casuists could properly dispose of such ascription. If a sin, it is a sin against God, against the Kingdom of Heaven; nevertheless a sin which arises from an absolute error of judgment, a misapprehension of what God intends, of what God's truth actually is. Israel must view Stern, Friedman, and Zolli as having sinned grievously in becoming converts, through a presumption of judgment.

To be born a Jew is, if we accept the meaning of religious history, no accident. It is a providential occurrence, for God intends something by birth. Granted that the order of nature proceeds with relative independence of the interruption of God; yet the prevision of God which orders the contours of history prepares the way of Providence, for God acts on his will and concretizes his intentions. To be born a Jew is, therefore, a consequence of divine will. To be a Jew, to take the fact of birth and draw from it its meaning, is not easy. The Jew must unfold the chrysalis of his birth. If he deny it he denies Providence, he turns away from the path of Providence into another. This other way may also express the intention of Providence, but it is not the way appointed for him. The individual Jew may leave Israel for the Christian world. As I have indicated, such defection must be viewed as a crucial misapprehension of the will of God, a decisive error of judgment. It is not a sin against Israel, the people, because the community remains to keep faith with God's promise to Abraham. It is a sin against God because it makes claim to know better of God's will than man is capable. Theologians are justly sensitive to man's pretensions to know the activity of grace. We may discern the signs of grace, but to know the inner rhythm of grace eludes us. So the convert, whom Israel must view as having succumbed to the fruits of misapprehension. The decision of the convert is inescapably an excess, a distortion. The error of judgment consists in having taken the word of God, given to Israel in the desert, and carried it out from amidst the people, removed it from the experience that gave it texture, the experience of the people. He who removes from the life of Israel the Word and makes of it *his* word, his private word, cannot help but distort it.

Jesus comes as the single man from Galilee and addresses the people out of his own heart, appropriating the Word as his word. Israel cannot but view his speech as a distortion of Providence, for the word that is intended to be carried as a moving treasure of the people is made the object of individual appropriation. The sin of Jesus is the sin of misappropriation.

Up to the moment that the Word of God is spoken at Sinai, the meetings of God and man have been essentially spatial, for God has spoken to the individual man alone. The individual carries his space with him as he moves, and the Word of God is carried by him as a parcel of space. As the Patriarchs wandered, single and alone, the Word of God became their own, for them alone to speak and bequeath. It was their private possession, higher in kind and quality than their goods and chattels, but of a piece with goods and chattels, for the Word was rooted to their subjectivity, privacy, and individuality. It is not unusual that Christian thinkers, in the image of that singular and unique spatializer of the Word, should claim more unambiguously as their own the Patriarchs than either Moses or the prophets. The

Patriarchs are, like Jesus, pilgrims of faith, without community, yet seeking one. The Patriarchs are, indeed, exemplary models for the believer; yet without the regulative role of the community they can as easily wither as unfold the subjectivity of the spirit. The individual can only spatialize the Word; but the myriads of individuals that encounter God at one moment, whether at Sinai or in the liturgy, cannot spatialize the Word, for the God they carry away addresses not the individual, in his singularity and loneliness, but all of history.

The mystery of revelation is that God chooses to speak not to the single man, but to human history. No longer to the Patriarchs or to Moses alone, but to the whole people, and not merely the collective people, but to the individuality that is defined out of the single man and the community as they are bound together and interact in the same moment. For when God speaks to six hundred thousand he takes his word in jeopardy, for this Word, if misappropriated to space, is liable to distortion. When the individual carries away such a word, that word becomes his property, his space; yet when God risks his word to a people, he stakes his destiny in time. It is the consummate risk that he consigns the Word to a people. Though every man carry away the Word for himself as before, there are now millions of others who do likewise. Inevitably they limit and qualify each other and build out of the common life with the Word an organic sensitivity to God's speech. This is how the Word of Israel ceases to be only a promise to the Patriarchs and becomes the community of Israel. The people confirm the reality of revelation. It is for this reason that the critical center of revelation is not allowed to the trustworthy rendition of Moses, but is spoken aloud to the people and graven on tablets of stone. Similarly it is for this reason that when the Word is spoken, not to the people, but to the single individual, the people must not trust that Word. It is not attested to, therefore its validity is suspect. This is the innermost source of our assertion that Karl Stern, John Friedman, and Israel Zolli have sinned against Providence, the Word, the community of Israel, and the coming of the Messiah.

# The One-Way Bridge:
## 1955 and 1956/1957

*The Bridge*,[1] edited by Father John Oesterreicher, is the first of a projected series of annual publications of the Institute of Judaeo-Christian Studies. The first volume has modest pretensions. Monsignor John McNulty, in introducing it, speaks repeatedly of its exploratory character: the reconnoitering of the common ground of Israel and Christianity, its agreements and disagreements on fundamental issues of eschatology and salvation, its common patrimony. All is seen however *sub specie Christi*. The writers are Christian, whether by birth or persuasion. Many are ecclesiastics. All are passionately concerned with the dissident house of Israel. The essays which make up the volume cover vast and frequently treacherous waters. Many of the contributors, like Raissa Maritain, the Abbot of Downside, and Father Oesterreicher, are well known; however, other names are considerably more obscure, and it is not quite clear what qualifies them to participate, other than affection and good will for the common enterprise. The subjects are as diffuse as the contributors are varied, covering Biblical theology, Marc Chagall, Shylock, Abraham Heschel, the Finaly case, the Jewish Burial Service, and reviews of works by Martin

1. *The Bridge: A Yearbook of Judaeo-Christian Studies,* Volume I, edited by John M. Oesterreicher, Pantheon Books, New York, 1955.

Buber (fair), Victor Gollancz (highly sympathetic), and Robert Graves (comes off poorly).

All in all, it is not easy to read *The Bridge* without irritation. The essays are either apologetic or polemical. Where they intend instruction, it is highly dubious what they are intended to instruct: Jewish intransigence or Christian ignorance. Throughout there runs the multifibered cord of Olympian condescension, Christian reverence for mysterious Israel, and pious indignation at Jewish stubbornness. It is a dreadfully uneven volume. To review it is, therefore, extraordinarily difficult.

I shall not concern myself with minor responses—the temptation to be ironic or slighting. Since it is irritation which more generally describes my reaction, let me try to state its source.

History has fashioned for Israel, during the past two decades, a destruction which has all but decimated its physical presence. If we, in our youth, aspired to power and dominion, we have been disabused of such ambition. Israel did not conquer the nations— at least not visibly. Spiritually, it is but the barest remnant; today but a remnant of the remnant, for the community of Israel is sundered and broken. We might, were this sufficient to the character of Israel, blame ourselves for what has befallen us and be silent, but such would be but one half of the character of Israel. At the same moment that the prophets denounce the sins of Israel and proclaim the justice of her downfall, they make known the guilt of Egypt, Syria, and Babylon. At this moment there are no prophets among us. We must be both our own and the world's prosecutors. There is, on this account, savor in the Psalmist's plea for revenge—a savor which, though I do not wish to enjoy it, results nevertheless from such vital passion, such uncompromising delight in justice that it impels us to seek judgment; on occasion, to force it from heaven. Our speech, being unequal to the power of the Psalmist's, must rest content with pale versions of the same passion. We can but ask if Rome, for all its love for Israel, is as well contrite for what it did not do for Israel. The speeches of random cardinals were nothing against the fury of the past decades. Does the Vicar of Christ, for all his love, weep for his spiritual brothers (*The Bridge* bears as its motto the statement of Pius XI: "Abraham is called our Father. Spiritually we are Semites")? This is all that we can ask. This is our single plea: that the Church of Rome make confession for its profound and unforgettable indifference. There is excommunication for heresy. Is there no excommunication for murderers? If there is none, one might at least insist that there be contrition for having countenanced murder.

The foregoing statement of conviction is material to any understanding of why *The Bridge*, as an effort to speak of the Christ to Israel, must fail.

All of the writers in *The Bridge* repeatedly ask Israel to please forget history. Wipe the slate, they plead, and let us start afresh. The fundamental fact which such writers must learn is this: we are nothing as Israel without history. Forget history and we forget our wisdom. For what is our past, present, and anticipation if it is not history? We begin history with Abraham, center history at Sinai, and end history at a moment not yet at hand. Since the consummation of history is not upon us, we can know history only through the seriousness of the moment. This is the core of the paradox which none of the writers in *The Bridge* recognizes: Israel cannot forget history, cannot ignore the enormities of Christendom because history is *not* redeemed. To be redeemed, that is, to transcend history to God, is to acknowledge that the Messiah has come. Obviously the only way to attend to the Christian message—to forget history in the divine forgetfulness of a fulfilled redemption—is to be Christian. We are not Christian. We know no transformation of the historical moment. For this reason we cannot forget the history of our anguish before Christendom.

The history of Israel before Christendom, its attitude of constant, but pathetically ineffective indignation, is but the postlude to the rejection of Jesus. It is, therefore, central that the essay of Hilaire Duesburg, "The Trail of the Messiah," be considered more closely. Father Duesburg challenges Israel to define its rejection of Jesus. Indubitably the claim of the Church is more easily rejected than the claim of Jesus to be the Christ. Who is this being who acknowledges himself to be Messiah of Israel and King of the Jews? If he is not the Messiah, can Israel answer who is? This is precisely the point which Christians miss. We cannot, nor is it incumbent upon us, to answer. It is sufficient to say that Jesus is not he whom we expect. Were we to see with the eyes of Christian faith, we would know what it means to be redeemed. Again the paradox of belief: to believe is to affirm as fact what others cannot perceive with the mere eye of reason. The problem is intensified, however, when the encounter of Judaism and the Christ occurs, for we too see with the eye of faith and yet we deny that what is promised us has come. Our only criterion is this: he who comes to redeem us comes out of the community of Israel and cannot speak to us except through that community. The Messiah, in being the Anointed, is born out of the community and addresses the community with the Word that is of Israel. Jesus comes as the single man from Galilee and addresses the people out of his own heart, appropriates the Word as his own word. He cannot help but confuse and distort. He freezes the Word where the Word is intended, as in the Ark that David bore to Jerusalem, to be carried as a moving treasure. Up to the moment that the Word of God is spoken at Sinai, the meetings of God and man have been essentially spatial, for God has spoken to the individual man alone. The individual carries his space with him, and the Word is carried by him as his property, as a parcel of space. The myriads of individuals that encounter God at one moment, whether at Sinai or in the synagogue, are both individual and community in one. He who will address history with the perfect Word that is both the one and the many at each moment redeems history, for he makes of it the community that imitates God. It is the presumption of Jesus to have set himself before the community as its rebuke, to have renounced the criterion of history which measures Israel only as holy people, never as holy person alone.

Roman Catholics, with whom I have spoken, are of two minds about the prospective dialogue of Christians and Jews. On the one hand, they are deeply and justifiably dismayed by the ignorance of Christianity displayed by most Jews. To correct this they seek communication. On the other hand, they are reluctant if not incapable of creating the conditions of reciprocal communication. As one Catholic thinker expressed it to me recently: "There are fundamental issues about which communication is impossible." He paused and added, somewhat piteously, "Unfortunately these issues are the most important." Presumably he meant that Catholics could not, in all seriousness, be open to the inescapable Jewish denial of Jesus Christ, could not seriously countenance such statement. If so, then communication is indeed impossible. *The Bridge* is admittedly one-way communication. Its intention is to enlighten the Catholic and lubricate Jewish inflexibility. Nowhere does the Jew speak.

It is indispensable if there is to be communication that the Christian allow himself openness before the Law, which determines the Jewish response to the "fulfilled" Christ. Where Israel, possessing the Law, awaits the Messiah, Christians claim to have consummated the Law in an already achieved redemption. There can be no communication unless this reciprocity is acknowledged.

*The Bridge*, under the editorship of John Oesterreicher (a veteran warrior of the Jewish-Christian dialogue), is a distinguished effort which encourages the kind of one-sided discussion that Christianity has enjoyed for centuries. It is hoped that this kind of discussion illumines Christians (such essays as that of M. Thaddea de Sion on the Jewish burial liturgy surely will). Such a one-way bridge on which Jews are met, but do not meet, perpetuates, however, the conditions of the first century, where, in an obscure area of an obscure country, a movement of which no Jew took particular note shaped our destiny.

## II

I shall not review another volume of *The Bridge*. My review of the first volume raised certain dilemmas which a reading of the current volume confirms and strengthens. It is apparent, therefore, that my dilemmas were not accidents of judgment, but result from the essential character of *The Bridge*. It is, therefore, fruitless to repeat again and again what remains true once and for all. The "Bridge," which editor John M. Oesterreicher would build between Judaism and Christianity, is fixed and unalterable.

Israel is bade listen and not respond, be attentive, hear, and remain silent. Father Oesterreicher makes it clear in his Foreword to the present volume[2] that he, for one does not believe that it is necessary for the object of address to respond, as long as it is addressed as a "Thou." Presumably, Buber has become for Father Oesterreicher a coiner of metaphors—for Buber makes quite clear (and I could cite innumerable passages) that the Thou is spoken only where there is an acknowledgment of real presence and

2. *The Bridge* 1956/1957, Volume II, edited by John M. Oesterreicher, Pantheon Books, New York, 1956.

responsiveness, where there is awareness that the Thou must respond if there is to be a real relation. If Israel is not addressed in such fashion as to evoke answer, if the life of address does not command life, then Israel is not addressed with directness, power, or truth.

Since Catholic canon law inhibits the directness with which alone interfaith theological discourse can take place, it seems foolish to continue to operate as though *The Bridge* should be answered. If Father Oesterreicher is convinced that the Thou is spoken, he is entitled to his self-deception, but we should not be a party to it.

It is futile, I believe, to consider seriously and repeatedly a work which is based upon a fundamental and incorrigible misapprehension of its subject matter. The misapprehension of Israel, for Israel and the faith of Israel is the subject matter of *The Bridge*, is fundamental and incorrigible because it is founded upon a Christian theological appraisal of Judaism. This is as it should be. I do not object to clarity of perspective, to an articulate and structured frame of reference—it is indubitably better to be clear, than to be vague, in theology. There is a difference, however, between theological principle and apologetics. *The Bridge* has never been clear on this point. Its corresponding French organ, *Cahiers Sioniens*, or the Swiss Protestant organ, *Judaica*, differ from it radically in a number of respects: where the former is apodictic, the latter are exploratory; where the former combines serious study with the worst kind of religious journalism, the latter are unfailingly scholarly; where the former is apologetic, the latter are irenic. *The Bridge* speaks Thou, but makes clear that only in the reunion of Judaism and Catholicism can the Thou be spoken. *Cahiers Sioniens* and *Judaica* believe no differently, but begin with the assumption that Christianity must first rediscover Israel, before it can convert her. The attitude of the former makes for persistent defensiveness and consequent arrogance; the latter are authentically humble. *The Bridge* belabors its affection, love, charity for Israel; magnifies and extols her virtues; urges her with parental superiority to be virtuous and true and abandon her perfidy. The European journals print no such sentimental mush and are content with the hard facts of theological life.

In an effort to locate and define the characteristics of the fundamental misapprehension of Israel which makes discourse such as that of *The Bridge* meaningless and presumptuous, I re-examined both volumes of *The Bridge*. Two characteristics emerged: one, Biblical studies were generally superior, more judicious, and well-founded than studies of post-Biblical or historical Judaism; two, the quality of Catholic theological discussion of normative Judaism is indifferent, uninspired, and not particularly well informed. These observations should come as no surprise. The resurgence of Catholic interest in the Bible has produced a number of impressive and thoughtful Biblical theologians: Bonsirven, Lagrange, Tresmontant, Duesburg, Journet, to mention but a few. It is only natural that Catholic studies of the Hebrew Bible should make common cause with Jewish concerns: as long as the anagogic hermeneutics of the Rabbinic Age and the Patristics do not obtrude, both Catholic and Jew will share the conviction that the Hebrew Bible contains the record of a manifest, self-disclosing, and concerned God.

The Bible is, however, the *terminus a quo of* both Judaism and Catholicism. Out of the Bible comes the tradition; out of the Gospels comes the Church. Neither Jews nor Catholics remain self-sufficiently preoccupied with the Bible. The problematic difference is that where Jews consider the Church an erroneous, but well-intentioned, mistake to be corrected by God at the end of history, the Church considers itself the legatee of Israel, its historical judge and chastiser, and now, under the conditions of a secularism that makes for theological forbearance, its loving instructor. Where Judaism acknowledges the fact of Christianity as a real fact (however little it knows about it), Christianity does not really consider Judaism to have survived. As such, the survival of Israel is made a sign and witness, a testimony to historic guilt, a mystery. Israel is a theological device, a *ficelle* of Christian history —but she is not alive and independent.

*The Bridge* obviously suffers from the fact that Catholicism has never thought through a clear position regarding the survival and restoration of post-Biblical Judaism. The articles in the current volume dealing with rabbinic and historical Judaism testify to this: they are either routine statements of Jewish liturgical life glossed with apostolic emphases or unbearably sloppy readings of the subtle and ambivalent philo-Christianity of sculptor Jacob Epstein. Miss Bede reveals nothing to the Jew that the liturgy does not already make self-evident and the Süssmans, having no aesthetics and little more than theological enthusiasm, find it sufficient to claim that their own convictions are those which Epstein has made bronze and stone. What is the instruction? Whom does this instruct? For Jews or Catholics? None of these questions can be answered, because the Church has presently no frame of reference in terms of which to articulate the answer. As long as such clarity of perspective is lacking, the efforts of *The Bridge* will be indifferently successful—an occasional article (such as that of Quentin Lauer's on the Bible or J. Edgar Brun's review of Klausner's *The Messianic Idea in Israel*) will be rich and meaningful because Catholic theology is clear on both issues—but, on the whole, *The Bridge* will remain a boring and repetitious affair.

In sum, I think it would be advisable if Jews forgot about *The Bridge*. It may help Catholics to think more intelligently, in Catholic terms, about what little of Judaism Catholics know or care to understand. This is a laudable purpose and one which would justify the continued appearance of *The Bridge*.[3] But *The Bridge* cannot address Judaism unless it takes seriously that Judaism is, on its own terms, alive. I do not think that Judaism would be averse to discussing these terms—it did so under considerably more discouraging conditions at Barcelona and Tortosa, and it would be willing to do so again.

*The Bridge,* as it is and promises to remain, is open only for one-way traffic. It is destined, by its own unwillingness to encourage authentic discourse, to become progressively more boring and unoriginal—beating the same breast, thumping the same drum, singing the same love chant. Alas, the Jews are asked (and Father Oesterreicher justifies such a request) to sit in the audience, watch the show, and keep silent. There are two choices for a captive audience: applaud or sit on your hands.

3. Publication of *The Bridge* continues, a fifth volume having recently appeared.

# The Polemicist
## and The Professor

In *The Professor and the Fossil*[1] Maurice Samuel has addressed a trenchant reply to Arnold Toynbee's judgments on Jewish history and culture. Arnold Toynbee, though not replying to Samuel, has published *An Historian's Approach to Religion.*[2] A celebrated historian and a distinguished man of letters have turned their attention to problems of religion and, specifically, by virtue of the self-imposed limitation of Samuel's attack, to Jewish religion and its Christian outgrowth.

There is little, indeed, that one can add to Samuel's brilliant sally against this supposedly well-defended bastion of historical scholarship. He is but one of many Davids who have gone forth to war against this Goliath. Although Goliath has by now been slaughtered, his name survives in the salons of Gath. No single shot dropped him. He is the victim of multiple onslaughts, all directed to his clearly abundant weaknesses. Samuel has overseered the assault on but a single soft spot—Toynbee's analysis of the origin and history of the Jews. He makes pertinent use of avail-

1. *The Professor and the Fossil,* by Maurice Samuel, Alfred A. Knopf, New York, 1956.
2. *An Historian's Approach to Religion,* by Arnold Toynbee, Oxford University Press, New York, 1956.

able scholarship to indicate the misinformation and half truths involved in Toynbee's persistent confusion of the Hebrews with some vast society called, with proud obscurantism, "Syriac Civilization." The incompleteness of Toynbee's understanding of the Bible, his lack of familiarity with rabbinic tradition, his Christocentric biases, his consistent denigration of Diaspora Judaism, his incredible distortions of Zionism, his appalling lack of compassion, palpable hostility, and thinly veiled irritation with Judaism and Jewish survival are accurately and definitely nailed. What we have then in *The Professor and the Fossil* is a hotly argued, passionately felt, and telling indictment of a detractor and profound defense of Jewish existence and vitality.

It is clear, if one examines Toynbee's argument closely, that a single proposition is the core of his offense—it is the charge that Jewish civilization is a "fossil." It is justifiable that Samuel should feel offended. I should be equally offended were I to accept the judgment. Nobody relishes being thought moribund, arrested, frozen in the ice block of history. Let it be noted, at the outset, that Toynbee's judgment of Judaism is not unique. (Toynbee dislikes exclusiveness so much that not even fossildom should be an exclusive possession.) There are many arrested civilizations, many offshoots of primary cultures that failed to mature and adapt. In short, there are many fossils. Most of the great civilizations of the ancient world are fossils—Greece, Rome, Egypt. All made bequests to their legatees, but none survived and none has been properly resurrected. It is the misfortune of the Jew that he is a surviving fossil, the only surviving fossil in the West. (I wonder whether the Amish, Quakers, Millenarians, Levellers *et alter* are fossils: they are certainly arrested peoples. As a matter of fact, there are some modern fossils, just recently conceived—the Jehovah Witnesses, who are but latter-day Apocalyptists and the Christian Scientists, who have isolated St. Augustine's theory of evil and made a religion out of it.) The Jew is different. He is a big fossil. He is all over. He is troublesome, clever, effective, and now, it appears, quite warlike. Because he is such a vivacious fossil, he never disappears for an instant throughout *A Study of History*.

Having established for the moment my equal irritation with being a fossil, I must ask: aren't we? A man meets, for example, another in the street (one of whom he knew little directly, only hearing reports of him from hearsay or occasional gossip). He says to him, trying to walk around him: "Friend, you are a fossil." What should such a man do? Should he go through Shylock's speech about having blood, affections, loves, and hates just to prove that he is quite live and human? Toynbee would agree that he is quite live and human, but would insist, nevertheless, upon his fossildom.

Samuel, obviously goaded by the persistent repetition of this fundamental judgment, spends considerable space recounting the marvels of Jewish history, life, and letters. The uniqueness of Yiddish literature, the rebirth of Hebrew, the fundamental insights of Jewish religion, the nature of Zionism are explored. It is imagined that the force of exposure will conclusively demonstrate that the flame of life burns strong and consistent. Is such defense, however, to the point? Here is a historian who has pretended to know everything. It is clear that he does not, that his theories are poorly supported and his evidence weak at crucial points. What does this really matter? Another historian is exploded. What counts, I believe, is that there is a core of honest concern in Toynbee's work which underlies all that he has written—a preoccupation with the fate of civilization and the destiny of Western culture. All culture is assessed retrospectively from the vantage point of the present moment. Toynbee is fundamentally impervious to the exigencies of the past. He is concerned with what he sees around him—the breakdown of community, the disintegration of cohesive values, the triumph of technocracy, the reincarnation of violence. He sees, as practically everybody sees, that the West is shot through with weakness, that the East is on the rise, and that nothing may survive (in the event of the atomic war) if something is not done immediately. The passion of his historiography is to build up a version of the past which explains to his satisfaction why we have gotten to this pretty pass.

With such an overriding concern, it is clear that he should forget about Jews and Judaism, in a word, fossilize them. For some fifteen or sixteen centuries we have not been on the stage of world history. From the second to the tenth century, Nehardea, Sura, and Pumbedita, the Patriarchates and Gaonates of the world were the centers of Jewry. Little else transpired in the West (other than the consolidation of Catholic Europe and the decline of Byzantium as an original cultural center) during this period, but what little else did occur was marked by but peripheral contact with Judaism. With the exception of a brief period from the tenth to the thirteenth century, Jewry has had little vital or significant contact with the movement of ideas or power in Christendom or Islam. From the thirteenth century to the present, Judaism was a plant of the dark places, growing rich foliage, being seen by none but its faithful gardener. The triumph of emancipation and secularism gave rise to renewed Jewish contact with the West—but the contact was too little authentically Jewish and, according to Toynbee, too late (the tragedy was wrought in the triumph of technique and experimental science in the seventeenth century). Unfortunately, in the seventeenth century only Spinozas among Jews spoke good Latin.

Granting then Toynbee's fundamental concerns and premises, we are fossils. Granting his anti-Semitism, his hostility, his egregious oversights, his errors of fact, Judaism has still contributed little to lighten the burden of the West. Let us mark clearly what is being said: Toynbee does not see disembodied ideas of grandeur and ultimate vision sufficient to qualify a culture for permanent vitality. Toynbee does not deny the genius of the Hebrew Bible or Jewish monotheistic passion—all he says is that, from the accesses of historical judgment, these ideas were not carried through the life of the West by Jews, but by Christians. It is his contention that Judaism has not counted in the Christian world. I do not care, at this moment, to recount the valid reasons for the ineffectiveness of Judaism in the Christian world. They were sufficient to keep the Jews alive. They rationalize what little we need to have rationalized (just remember, we say, those repressive Papal Encyclicals, the forced conversions, the wiping out of Jewish communities, the economic disabilities, the enforced isolation). Such rationalizations are true and meaningful, but again beside the point. Toynbee is not concerned with the past as past, but only with the past as present and future. He acknowledges the dreadful repression of the Jews under Christendom. This is symptomatic, he admits, of the breakdown of Western Christianity, the witness to a corrupting secularization of the divine image of the Church. Since what counts is the future of the West, it is beside the point whether Jews have died from their own error and neglect or from the world's stupidity. They are dead. Their insistence upon survival is of no moment in the crucible of history, for their effectiveness in weighting the historical balance is measured in the living witness of ideas, spiritual conviction, and divine mission.

When it comes to answering this argument, it seems to me that Samuel is unprepared. Had he read *An Historian's Approach to Religion*, this side of the coin would have shone bright. It is precisely Toynbee's attitude toward religion that is interesting and significant. For if one attends to it closely, one finds a remarkable likeness in fundamental mood and attitude to that which Samuel expresses in his attack upon him. Naturally, Toynbee's confusion is Christian, where Samuel's is Jewish, but, *mutatis mutandis*, they both assume the same stance. I must honestly admit that I feel their enormous closeness, because I agree with neither of them. I think it is precisely Samuel's lack of clarity about religion which prevents him from really answering Toynbee in the only way that Toynbee should be answered. Samuel reminds me of Max Weber's great attack on Marx, which consisted of proving that, not economic factors, but sociological determinants foreordained the historical conduct of the proletariat and middle class. Weber shifted the elements but left the determinism unassailed. Samuel does likewise. He proves that Jewry is alive. Liveness, however, is not the issue. The issue is whether the vitality of Judaism had anything of moment to say to a Christian world and a history in need of help. He proved vitality to you and me, but whether he proved it to Toynbee I doubt.

Toynbee has, to say the least, a most ambivalent view of religion. He has defined the highest expression of religious truth as that which considers "Suffering [to be] the essence of Life; and, instead of trying to get rid of Suffering . . . tries to use it as an opportunity for acting on feelings of Pity and Love which it believes to be divine as well as human." This becomes the theoretical capstone for his approbation of Christianity and Mahayana Buddhism. The essential link between them is that they witness, so Toynbee believes, to the voluntary return of the *illuminati* from the perfect state of understanding (in which they could remain, viz., Hinayana Buddhism) into the degraded order of the world. The world is under the aegis of original sin, idolatry, and corruption. Though this triad of judgment upon the world is consistently appealed to throughout his analysis, Toynbee will, with equanimity, describe it as a mythology.

Western Christianity is averred to be the apogee of religious history, though it appears that there were few moments in Western Christianity that can really be approved—and those, precisely, when Christian hegemony was most insubstantial. The period prior to Constantine, the centuries of martyrdom and independence from temporal power, are those he admires. Toynbee admits regretfully, however, that the possession of truth requires that the self-defeating action of missionizing, temporal organization, and hierarchies, be employed. From them, he acknowledges, the excesses of religion result. He exhorts us to return to essentials, to fundamental visions, to the preinstitutional fraternities of believers. Where Toynbee is immensely moving in his description of the truth, he is almost childlike in his exposure of fanaticism, idolatry, and the secular perversions of the spiritual mission of religion. For a student of power (and secular history is but the examination of the disposition and effects of power), he is apparently appalled that power works the way he knows it works. When it comes to a positive recall to truth—he cannot choose, because choice involves the decision that one truth is truer than another, or, perhaps, even perfectly true. To make such a decision means apparently to resubmit man to the wheel of power. So we are left at the conclusion of *An Historian's Approach to Religion* with an exhortation "to believe in our own religion without having to feel that it is the sole repository of truth. We can love it without having to feel that it is the sole means of salvation." In the end we are to surrender to our own dim, inconclusive, and partial vision of the mystery. The mystery is all. The rest is commentary. Though ideally we should go away and study, it is clear that we have no time.

The net effect of Toynbee's view of religion is that at every moment in which religion really functioned integrally within the social order, the state, and the civilization of an era, it surrendered to idolatry and self-corruption. Whenever it was of the party of the distressed, alienated, and outcast, it made contact with the truth. This is a rather distressing historian's view of religion. Since we cannot really correct the corruptions of the religious order, we are bade to keep its ravages at a minimum—curb exclusiveness, abnegate absolutism, accept partiality, and be patient. Patient for what I am not sure, because Toybee does not talk of Messiah, Second Coming or anything else. There is no eschatological hope, no future redemption, no divine entrance into time expected.

Does Samuel give us greater hope for meaningful survival? With all the vitality and life that he demonstrates the Jews to possess, what are we supposed to do? I feel dressed and ready to go, but I don't know where. In a rather important chapter, "The Nature of Jewish Monotheism," Samuel notes: "One may properly say that Judaism is meaningless without the Jewish Bible, not because it tells of the discovery of God, but because it mirrors the struggle of recalcitrant man with the consequences of his discovery." This view is documented and expanded. An absolutely valid emphasis is placed throughout on the sacred character of Jewish history, the conditions of identity, the passion for study as a means of ascertaining the divine will. All well and good. But what is the task of Judaism before the world? It should be noted that what is stressed in *The Professor and the Fossil* is a fundamentally autonomous view of religion, a view distinctly at variance with the theonymous view that I believe ought to prevail. The mystery of Jewish history, Samuel seems to argue, does not lie in the utterly unpredictable and demanding activity of God upon Israel, but in the wonder of the people's response to God. Samuel is not alone in turning the emphasis of Jewish history from God's dealing with Israel to Israel's dealing with God. It is of a piece with the whole survivalist ethos which has motivated most of modern American Jewish theology. What mobilizes Jewish response is not the charge that God has deserted Israel (a charge made ever since the Crucifixion and a charge never properly answered) but the charge that Israel has deserted God. It is the problem of Jewish survival and not the quality of survival that occupies center stage. It is precisely this failure of orientation that leaves Samuel and Toynbee in fundamentally the same boat—holding fast to a religion with no articulated future, maintaining a view of religious truth without a complementary vision of religious vocation. Samuel acknowledges that the Jew who abnegates the specific elements of God-identification that define Jewry "secularizes himself out of his Jewish identity." What preoccupies me and obviously preoccupies Toynbee is, granting this God-identification, what is Jewry going to do about it here and now, in this moment of history?

Both Toynbee and Samuel, it seems to me, are left with the same thing: a religion that is too self-preoccupied and craven to take the risk of absolute validity. I grant that the terrors of such a position are great, but fanaticism, brutality, and corruption need not be the price mankind must endlessly pay for the conviction of truth. Judaism does have something to say to the West, but it must come forth into the West with a clear and articulate vision of the truth it has guarded secretly for centuries. In this way and only in this way is Toynbee really answered and the fossil truly revived.

# Moses, Mystery,
# and Jesus

In his essay on "The Dogmas of Judaism," Solomon Schechter sketches the history of the discussion that begins in earnest with Maimonides' Thirteen Articles of Faith. It is interesting to note that the opponents of Maimonides' credo challenge his historical dogmas—the primacy of Moses among the prophets, the immutability of the Torah, the doctrines of the Messiah and of resurrection—rather than his metaphysical "dogmas"—the existence, unity, incorporeality, and eternity of God. Truly we can speak with some philosophical clarity about God and nature but, unfortunately, with little philosophic clarity about the persistence and destiny of Israel. Properly speaking, "dogma" refers to belief not capable of being rationally exhibited, to primary mystery.

In Judaism, the primary mystery is the mystery of Torah and Israel, the historic dogmas of Maimonides' principles (6 through 13) of the Credo; this is the core of Jewish belief—a core essential to any religion, despite the disdain of modern Judaism for dogmatics—which can only be acknowledged, but never rationally set forth, for every statement of it leads to a theologically circular argument. The first five Maimonidean principles on the existence of God are subject to rational and analogical exposition, and thus accessible to the light of natural reason and demonstration.

In all, whether our principles be demonstrable or dogmatic, we cannot do without belief. Belief in the existence of a problem is the first belief. Unless man's world, history, destiny, and death be viewed as problematic, unexhausted by empirical and sociological explanations, there can be neither proof (of God) by natural reason nor acknowledgment of fundamental mysteries. We commence with faith in the meaning of the problem. Only then can we proceed to define the content of faith.

These preliminary reflections are called forth by the publication in France of *Moses: The Man of The Covenant*. The volume appears under the auspices of *Cahiers Sioniens*,[1] a review edited by Father Paul Demann, priest in the order of the Fathers of Zion.

*Moses* is a coherent collection of sixteen articles treating of the figure and work of Moses, as he is understood in Jewish, Apostolic, Patristic, Byzantine, Moslem traditions, and medieval art, liturgy, and speculation. The participants are, in many cases, distinguished scholars (Jean Daniélou, Louis Gardet); or otherwise learned theologians and scholars who, though less familiar to American readers, are obviously skilled, committed, and eloquent students of the relevant literature. A volume of this kind, written by Catholics (some of whom are converts from Judaism[2]), is extraordi-

---

1. The *Cahiers Sioniens*, which appeared three times yearly (it is no longer published regularly), "has as its objective the deepening of the understanding of the relations between the Church and Israel—the illumination of their common spiritual patrimony, the definition and promotion of a Christian attitude toward Judaism and Jews, the study, in an objective and comprehensive manner, of the history, tradition, and life of the Jews,— in order thereby to work toward a profound and authentic *rapprochement*, in the light of the fullness of the People of God." Cf. the discussion of *Cahiers Sioniens, Juifs Mes Frères*, Jean Toulat, Editions Guy Victor, pp. 215-17.

2. The notably talented Renée Bloch was killed in 1955 in the unprovoked Bulgarian assault upon an airplane bound for Israel. She was profoundly Christian, and, in spite of her comparative youth, was already learned in the aggadic and speculative Hebrew literature.

narily difficult to assess. There can be little caviling with facts. By and large, the knowledge of Biblical and Rabbinic doctrine is exemplary and well-documented from Hebrew sources, as well as the whole literature of Jewish scholarship. The fundamental issues are not, therefore, issues of fact. There can be none of the usual and justified claim of Christian ignorance of Jewish sources. The principal focus of any discussion of *Moses*, therefore, must be theological.

*Moses*, in the tradition of Christian scholarship, is not Biblical apologetics, but Biblical theology. The Jews form a link in the dogmatic presumptions of Christianity. Whether or not Jews are dogmatic in their convictions, our history is subject, nevertheless, to dogmatic reconstruction. We can either meet the convictions of dogma with the pliant historicism of modern Jewish scholarship, or clarify what we, in truth, believe to be our history and its ultimate significance in the order of salvation.

The fundamental question that *Moses* poses is this: although it is admitted that Moses is, *par excellence*, the liberator, founder, and leader of Israel, that there is no other like Moses in those specific properties in which Moses excels *as man*, is it not just to view Moses and the Law as both mediate instruments in the preparation of mankind for fulfillment in Christ? Moses and the Law are deemed to be necessary *propaedeutoi* in the history of salvation. As the French Augustinian, Hugh of St. Victor (1096–1141), wrote: "The course of this world unfolds in three successive periods. The first is the period of the law of nature, the second that of the written law, the third is the period of grace. The first flows from Adam to Moses, the second from Moses to Christ, the third begins with Christ and will be finished with the end of the world." Moses is seen as the mediate moment in the history of mankind, perfect in those faculties in which man may realize perfection, and incomparable in the historic role which man may be fitted by God to perform. He is, nevertheless, witness in his life to the incompletion which nature and Law, separated from grace, imply. He is subject to temper, he rebukes God, he is a sinner,[3] he is punished, he is refused entrance to the Holy Land, his grave is forgotten and unmarked. Moses exhibits all the wretched conditions of the flesh which mark man. Notwithstanding his admitted sanctity and perfection, he is still a man. He falls under the law of limitation to which creatureliness is subject, and his works fall under the criticism that they are suitable to but one finite moment in history to be transcended in the unfolding of providence.

The writers in *Moses* are consistent in holding that the life of Moses may not be understood other than through its parallel to the unfolding of Christ and the Church. Without the Christ, Moses is evidently ill-suited to assume the illustrious role which he performs in Christian thought. Renée Bloch, in her study of Rabbinic literature, is faithful to the Hebrew text when she describes the many passages in the Midrash that interpret the vicarious suffering of Moses on behalf of Israel, the intermediary role of Moses, the attitude of Moses interceding for Israel through prayer and petition, the pastoral function of Moses, the messianic characteristics which Moses illustrates, the secret suffering, death, and burial-place of Moses. All appear to her, however, in the light of Christian thought, as exemplary indication that Moses is, in himself, living out the providential witness to the Christ.

In two other studies, those of Albert Descamps on "Moses in the Gospels and the Apostolic Tradition" and Paul Demann on

3. In her article, "Moses in the Rabbinic Tradition," Renée Bloch cites Deut. R. 2, 7, and 8; Petirat Mosheh, pp. 116, 117, 2nd ed., ed. Jellinek in Bet-ha-Midrash I, pp. 115-129.

"Moses and the Law in the Thought of Saint Paul," the issue moves from that of prophetic exegesis to direct challenge. In the Gospels and Apostolic literature, didactic and rhetorical argument emerge. Moses disappears as a sacrosanct figure (although he will reappear as such in the Patristic literature when Christianity is consolidated, and the Jerusalemite faction has been crushed by Paul). He is, during the Gospel interval, the representative figurehead of the Pharisees, and as such identifiable in spirit and act with the "curse of the Law." As Descamps notes, two parallel themes emerge in the Gospels: the transcendence of the Law in Christ, and the opposition between Moses and the Messiah. Jesus emerges as an interpreter of the Law, whose interpretations, however unprecedented, are considered greater than those of Moses[4]. He can break the Law, for he transcends it. He is the new Law. The old Law is dead. Whatever obedience he pays to it is, therefore, the respect of the Master for an older teacher to whom he is superior. It is, therefore, somewhat confusing to have Paul Demann, in his study of Paul, confuse the issue with constant attempts to show that Paul held the Law to be good and holy, while arguing at the same time what is patently clear from the Epistles, that Paul believed the Law to kill, to be of the reign of guilt, flesh, and death, to be of the dominion of slavery and servitude; whereas Christ is freedom, spirit, truth, salvation, and eternal life.

St. Paul in his Epistle to the Galatians writes: "If righteousness is through the Law then Christ has died for nothing." This cli-

---

4. Yehezkel Kaufman, in his masterpiece *Golah v'Necbar*, argues with considerable strength that the halakhic interpretations of Jesus, far from being novel, represent the documented view of one element of the Pharisees who, standing in the Hillelite tradition, argued from the perspective of the poor and dispossessed classes of society.

mactic observation may be considered the epigraph of *Moses*. If indeed salvation may still be obtained within the House of Israel, then assuredly Jesus the Christ died for nothing; moreover, it may then be argued with considerable force that Jesus was not the Christ, that he was but another false messiah.

Father Demann illuminates the Pauline position clearly when he comments: "Paul, the Christian, depends upon the Christ. He is no longer able to adhere to the Law. If the Law had been a simple moral and ritual legislation, even divinely given, one would be able to adhere to the Christ while keeping the Law with all its significance. But, and this is the grandeur of the Law which Paul recognized too well, it is much more than simple moral and ritual legislation. It was the center of the religious life of Israel, it had an exclusive function to mediate between God and his people, it was constitutive of the people of God . . . For this reason it could not be juxtaposed with the Christ . . . The Law and the Christ are certainly juxtaposed in the unity of a divine plan, but successively, not simultaneously."

If the Law saves, Christ dies for nothing. If the Law does not save, then Israel labors in vain. Ultimately the issue is that simple. The many hundreds of pages of *Moses* illustrate clearly that this has been the situation throughout the history of Christian thought: Law or Christ, not both.

What does Israel do in the face of such challenge? I am appalled by the thought that it does nothing, that it plies its way through history, correcting its texts, discerning the lines of its private past, unmindful that it is called upon to play a role in world history. If this is the case—dismal as the prospect seems—then clearly Christianity has won by default, for its challenge has gone without response. I would prefer to think that Israel "does not sleep nor slumber."

It is apparent that, in the formulation of dogmatic principles,

Jewish thought has been motivated by two distinct desires: the desire for order and coherence, and the desire to counter what Maimonides calls "the imitating creeds" of Christianity and Mohammedanism. Schechter employs the latter explanation to interpret Maimonides' inclusion in his Thirteen Articles of the principle of Moses' superiority to all prophets. One may argue, with due respect to Maimonides, that his formulation is somewhat beside the point, since Christianity does not deny that Moses is the greatest of the prophets. It asserts only that Moses prophesied another, who is of God under the accident of flesh. Moses may be prophet, but what of the absolute character of the Law? It is here that the much more critical assertion is made: the Law is given by God and may neither be added to nor diminished in any respect. Let us assume that such a proposition, though subject to interpretation and proper understanding, is formally correct. Is this not considerably more significant in countering the claim of Christianity than the superiority of Moses to other prophets? A more proper formulation of the dogma of Moses is this: Moses alone is chosen to announce the Torah. All other prophets differ from Moses in kind, for where others but confirm the Torah, he alone proclaims it. In this way Moses is made, not the greatest of the order of prophets, but different from the order of prophets. Not to deny his humanity, but to declare its superlative manifestation, is to affirm a dogma. Such statement is not available to demonstration, but to faith alone, for it affirms the unique providence of God, the mystery of his election and choice. I am not attempting to make pronouncement, but to indicate the kind of problem that makes the reassessment of the issue of dogmatics so critical. Many are the Jews who succumb to Christian doctrine, not through having believed in Christ and repudiated the Law, but having repudiated the Law only to discover that their repudiation is shared by Jesus Christ. If, indeed, Judaism is only the religion of good conscience, then it is nothing. Presumably we reject Jesus Christ because we destroy his claim by its contravention of infallible doctrine. If our doctrine is fallible or if we have no doctrine, I believe Judaism as religion is lost. If our survival is dependent upon our good sense and filial affection, we are more profoundly lost, for we shall survive on sentiment, not truth.

Can the Bible be interpreted as a prophetic document? Is it ever legitimate to take a document of literal history and discern concealed beneath its visible structure an invisible history? The Biblical literature is either explicitly or implicitly prophetic: explicitly, when the text actually prophesies events; implicitly, when it describes the consequences which may be expected from man's action and conduct. Certainly the prophecies of Isaiah and Jeremiah, as all the other prophets, are explicit. This is not to say that the language of explicit prophecy is literal. It may well be that the prophetic literature is direct, declarative, and unambiguous. It is equally possible, however, that it propounds a mystery which yields only to faith. Assuming that the Bible is prophetic in the sense that it discloses the reaches and unfolds the destiny of Israel, its prophetic character is still confined within the borders of the Jewish religious experience. The Christian exegete comes to the Bible with a single premise: Jesus of Nazareth is a Jew; given, therefore, the acknowledged prophecy of a Messiah contained in Jewish literature, and given the belief that the promised Messiah is Jesus, then the anticipations of Jewish literature and the realization of Christian faith are the same. From this view, all Jewish literature may be submitted quite consistently and justifiably to the analogical exegesis of Christian criticism. All that the Christian critic does is supply the missing term to Jewish prophecy: the name of the Messiah. This constitutes one form of Christian exegesis. The other form, typological criticism, is to find in the

Bible parallelisms to events in the life of Jesus and the Church. Thus the rock of Horeb, which Moses does not believe to contain water, is understood by Augustine and many other Church fathers to represent the obduracy of the Jews before the sacrament of baptism and the parallel claim of Peter and Jesus. The rock becomes the pivot image which supplies the link. It converts, as well, literal statement of the Bible into a prophetic admonition of future events.

*Moses* is not, therefore, apologetics in the formal sense. It is not the work of Christians intent on converting Jews. It is a profoundly challenging work, for it illustrates the incredible weakness of the Jewish position in the modern world. We are ill-prepared to meet with equal directness the challenge of such exegesis. There is only one answer: Jesus is not the Messiah awaited by Israel, prophesied by Scripture, or promised by Jewish doctrine.

I would not attempt here to redefine what I have argued elsewhere, that Jesus is not the Christ because he destroys the one organ of religious understanding that is essential before anything: the community of Israel. I argue only that, given the community, it must be known what the community believes itself to be. If it has no unique and unambiguous character, then it can be altered, and presumably, in principle, cease to be a Jewish community and become a Christian one. We do not deny that Christianity imitates Israel, but we affirm, by the doctrine of imitation, that Israel is the model and Christianity the copy. To be a model requires that principles of harmony, order, wisdom, and truth be exposed. More than such principles of reason, it requires that the ineluctable character of any perfect order be discerned: its sense of mystery. The Law, for all its folioed clarity and endless commentary, is mysterious—not in its ramification, but in its mere givenness. The fact that Israel is elected, that Moses is chosen to transmit that election, that the Torah defines the dimensions of that election, is the mystery. This is the heart of Jewish dogmatics. All else, the Messiah, the end of days, the resurrection of the dead, are but the consequences of having ordered history through Torah.

# Semite According
# to the Flesh

IN RECENT DECADES Roman Catholicism has achieved a level of
sophisticated familiarity with Jewish theological and liturgical life
which is remarkable after centuries of indifference and hostility.
To be sure, Protestantism also has been attentive to Judaism, but
its interest has been missionary and little more—witness the signal
failure, for example, of the World Council of Churches' 1954
Assembly to formulate any theological statement regarding the Jews.
From the point of view of Judaism, therefore, the Protestant witness, narrowly Biblicistic and evangelistic as it is, has been of
small consequence.

Roman Catholic concern for Judaism tends, however, to be
egregiously narcissistic. Being closed to free theological discourse
with the Jew, Roman Catholicism sets up a hothouse image of
Judaism. Such closet-theologizing has now produced an article,
"Spiritual Semites," by Thurston N. Davis, S.J.[1]—which de-
serves scrutiny, not only for the image of Judaism which it pro-
jects, but for the curious understanding of Jewish history which
it reveals.

1. *America*, Aug. 3, 1957.

*I*

It is Father Davis's thesis that Jew and Catholic, sharing a common spiritual ancestry and historical continuity, have links which ought to bind them together on the American scene. Implicitly, he argues that these links should be strengthened and made articulate, because both Jew and Catholic face a Protestant majority and a rampant secularism which threaten their common foundations. Jews and Catholics are adjudged intellectuals, respecters of reason and history (authority and tradition). Both share "fidelity to the one true God," though the Jews reject the new dispensation of Jesus Christ.

However, Father Davis asserts, the Jews have succumbed more than Roman Catholics to the temptations of the normalizing culture of the United States, have relaxed their grasp on their eschatological vision, have adjusted all too completely. Where they ought to stand together with Roman Catholics, they have given way to the erosions of a democratic secularism. Father Davis closes on a note of affection and admiration. Though the Jew continued to puzzle and occasionally to provoke the Catholic, he is to be looked upon "with understanding and even fondness" as "our historic brother."

Pope Pius XI once called Roman Catholics "spiritual Semites." This formulation has supplied Catholic apologists with an apparently inexhaustible bag of clichés. For what really is a "spiritual Semite"? Father Davis confuses the issue at the outset by affirming that the Catholic, in "contemplating the features of his Lord Jesus Christ, of the Mother of God or of the first saints and bishops of his Church, sees in them the beloved faces of Jews."

But is this not vision according to the flesh (presuming, of course, that popular liturgical art reveals anything at all, much less authentic Semitic lineage)? If it is vision according to the flesh, then much more in the history of the Jew divides him from than binds him to his Christian brother. It ought not to be forgotten that it is according to the flesh that Jews have suffered at the hands of Christendom. If, however, vision according to the spirit is meant, then surely Protestants, and not Roman Catholics alone, are "spiritual Semites," for they also claim the patrimony of Hebrew Scripture.

It would appear that Father Davis has spoken mildly and without rancor. But mildness and civility do not obscure the lines of confusion which streak his thesis. My objections (and no doubt the objections of a Protestant critic) lie, not with the substance of the argument, but with its principles, its unarticulated assumptions, which conceal its implicit presumption.

American Protestantism is dismissed out of hand as having no compassing vision of the historical past. "Unlike Jew or Catholic, the American Protestant finds it difficult to think himself back beyond his native religious origins. Everything that took place, religiously speaking, before Jamestown, the *Mayflower*, William Penn or Mary Baker Eddy appears to him to be something which happened to 'foreigners,' not to the American Protestant or to anyone he knows." If there is truth here, it is half truth at best. Protestantism does not consider itself disinherited. The patrimony of the apostles and the early fathers, the medieval church, the writings of the Reformers constitute a tradition—not, to be sure, a tradition normalized by authority and transmitted with univocality, but a tradition nevertheless. What distinguishes Roman Catholicism and Judaism from Protestantism is not the presence and seriousness of history, but an established hermeneutics which orders the rhythm and accent of history. Not history but theory of history separates Protestantism from Rome in this regard. To say more than this is obfuscating.


## II

As to the confraternity of historical fortune which Father Davis adduces as the bond between Jew and Catholic, his argument leaves much to be desired. The vicissitudes which befell Jew and Christian alike in the early days of Christianity were common only by virtue of the agency of martyrdom: Rome. The difference is profound. One day the agency of martyrdom would become, not Rome, but the church. The Jew can view both Rome and the church, according to both flesh and spirit, as oppressors.

The centuries-long era of "coexistence in Spain" which Father Davis next suggests as an example of the Judeo-Catholic experience has already been acknowledged by him to be an oversimplification (*Time*, September 2). His quotation from R. Trevor Davies's *Golden Treasury of Spain: 1501–1621*, to the effect that prior to the expulsion of the Jews from Spain in 1492 there were peace and fellowship between Christian, Mohammedan, and Jew, is questionable history. The first Mohammedan massacre of the Jews (500 families were slain) occurred in Granada in 1066. The pogroms of 1391 in Cordova, Seville, Toledo, Majorca, and throughout Christian Spain claimed tens of thousands of Jewish lives.

The fate of the Spanish Jews from the late fourteenth century until their expulsion was one of harassment, forced conversion, imprisonment, exile, or death. The toleration of medieval Spain, so far as it existed at all, reflected the cultural and financial dependence of the nobility upon the Jew (as the mediator of Mohammedan culture and trade) more than the forbearance of the medieval church. The peace and fellowship were not between Jew and Christian but between the Jew and Christendom. Needless to say, Father Davis has no examples of historical toleration and community after the close of the Middle Ages.

The foreshortening of history to its medieval perspective presses Father Davis's argument precipitously into the modern period. There, it is assumed, the argument is proved: American Catholics and American Jews share a "number of common points of view." It is true that there are superficial temperamental and sociological resemblances between American Catholics and American Jews. Those that Father Davis cites are, however, slight and transparent. He claims, for example, that there is "a historical Jewish-Catholic respect for the intellect and for the tradition of reason." This may be so—although it is the kind of point that leaves me cold; but it is certainly not proved by pointing to the prodigious knowledge of scholastic philosophy possessed by Harry A. Wolfson of Harvard.

## III

History disposed of and common foundations demonstrated, Father Davis proceeds to the real issue at hand. It is here that he is most perceptive and most wrong. The community of spiritual Semites aside, what is obvious is that the Jews are linked to Roman Catholics, and to Christianity *in extenso,* by the most tenuous and ambiguous of connections. The debt of Christianity to Judaism is profound—there is a Christo-Jewish tradition. It is questionable whether there is a Judeo-Christian tradition to which I could subscribe. All that *terra communa* which is designated the Judeo-Christian tradition is ruled by natural law. The common fidelity to the "one true God" which Father Davis cites exists; but it is only the enlightenment of the natural law and those all too brief accesses of providential grace which have kept us from each other's throats throughout history. The "mutual fidelity to the one true God" is so vague and imprecise a formula as to count for little. Good will, civil authority and, in the United States, the First and Fourteenth Amendments have counted for more in the long run.

The issue is joined, however, in Father Davis's admirably direct assertion that, in spite of the link of monotheism, the Jews reject Christ, the New Israel, and the church. He does not labor this point but proceeds immediately to a penetrating diagnosis of the corrosive acculturation of American Judaism—which, quite rightly, he feels has caused the Jew to lose touch with his historic religiosity, his eschatological passion, his awareness of the agony of the Exile.

The Jew, now acclimated and adjusted, no longer hangs together as he should with his Catholic brother. The Jew is trapped by the neurosis of self-preoccupation, looking out for his own welfare, seeking to ensure and protect his hard-won security on the American scene. Where the Catholic, Father Davis observes, is "open-ended" to the world, the Jew tends to consider only the fortunes of the Jew. The examples Father Davis cites as evidence of the Jewish disinclination to cooperate are the Hildy McCoy Ellis case, the objection of the American Jewish Congress to the inclusion of the religious question in the decennial census for 1960, and the Jewish opposition to religious instruction in the New York public school system. I shall attempt to discuss the first two points; the last is so thorny and involved that it would require a vastly more complex argument.

## IV

It is true that Jewish religious leaders were, without exception, silent on the Hildy McCoy Ellis case. I must note, however, that many distinguished Jewish leaders with whom I talked considered the position of the Roman Catholic plaintiff sound and justified. Moreover, it can be assumed that the Jewish community would have reacted as did the Roman Catholic community if the situation had been reversed. This acknowledged, it ought to be quickly observed that the pro-Catholic reaction of responsible and sensitive Jewish leadership would not have been echoed in the general Jewish community. There is the unavoidable and painful fact that many Jews doubtless felt deep satisfaction that the Jewish defendant had triumphed, that Christian protest had been without avail. The Jew remembers (wrongly perhaps) as the Christian forgets (wrongly perhaps) the Mortara case and hundreds of cases like it where events turned out the other way— Jewish children forcibly baptized and kidnapped. Nor ought it be forgotten that Jewish agencies are still trying to convince many European monasteries to give up Jewish children whom they sheltered during the war and now wish to preserve as Catholics.

More than this, however, there is surely room for Jewish prudence. It is often argued by Catholic thinkers, rationalizing the silence of the church on some issue considered pressing in the world, that the church must on occasion observe the discretions of prudence, deeming silence in such situations to be wiser than public declaration. Similarly, the Jewish community was protected from dissension and serious split by the prudential silence of Jewish religious leadership on the Hildy McCoy Ellis case. Silence, however, does not mean agreement with the decision of the courts.

Regarding the inclusion of the religious question in the census, the position of the Jewish community is equally justified. By contrast it ought not be thought, as Father Davis would have us think, that there was unanimity in Roman Catholic circles. In point of fact, the *Commonweal* came out against the inclusion of the religious question. Its reasons are mine as well. Though the information that the census questioning of religious affiliation might provide would be valuable for sociological and statistical research, it would have the effect of normalizing the interest of the federal government in the religious beliefs of its citizens. It is not the province of the government so to interest itself or to act neutrally to make such information available to others. Any incursion of government, however mild, into the field of religion is an unwarranted precedent. The religious freedom which Jews enjoy in the United States is such that, whatever my own eschatological pessimism, it is worth protecting even in an issue as trivial and circumstantial as this one.

Father Davis has written a symptomatic article. Though the era of good feeling is not yet over, it is thinning considerably. The Jew is neither reliable nor predictable as supporter or, *faute de mieux*, as ally of Roman Catholicism in the United States. This is in large measure due to the deplorable secularization of the Jewish community, to the disproportionately important power and influence of Jewish defense agencies, and to the lack of clarity in Jewish religious thought. If one could define the situation at the moment it is: inner ferment surrounded by an impenetrable core of self-protection. The Jew wants to protect what he and all Americans enjoy under the Constitution. At the same time he is rethinking his religious foundations. This situation creates a paradox: as a religious creature, the Jew should be profoundly skeptical of what he seeks to ensure and protect as an American.

It is my own conviction that the Jew is in Exile, but that he ought not for that reason to consider the state of Israel his refuge and homeland. There has always been in Jewish tradition the double vision of Israel—the terrestrial and the celestial Israel, the Israel of history and the Israel that shall arise at the end of days. That one Israel is of history and the other of eternity does not make me, and every Jew, any the less a child of the Exile. As long as the Divine Presence wanders in Exile, so do I. I am bound, therefore, to question the securities of time, to wonder at the assurances of secular power, to query professions of support and love whether they come to me by the law of the land or by the assertion of my age-old oppressors. Alas, I am an eschatologist and must pay the price of my eschatology—if one say to me that he whom I await has come I may love him as a human being, but I share no history with him. His is transformed and mine is not.

It comes to this: Father Davis may be a Semite according to the spirit, but Abraham is mine according to the flesh.

# III. Actualities and Possibilities

# The Jewish-Christian
# Contradiction

IN THE ANCIENT Good Friday liturgy of the Catholic Church, in the midst of incessant pleadings for all conditions of men, the following prayer is offered: "Let us pray for the unbelieving Jews: that our God and Lord will remove the veil from their hearts, so that they too may acknowledge our Lord Jesus Christ . . . Almighty, eternal God, who does not withhold Thy mercy even from Jewish unbelief, heed the prayers we offer for the blindness of that people, that they may acknowledge the light of Thy truth, which is Christ, and be delivered from their darkness: through the same Lord, Jesus Christ. Amen."

Not alone in receiving the attentive solicitude of the Church, the Jews are thus singled out for unique compassion.

Needless to say, I am under no illusion that the Catholic Church would alter its liturgy[1] to conform to the reigning unbelief of contemporary culture. But that she should continue, in this age of "tolerance" and religious disinterest—a time when religion has become increasingly popular as it has become increasingly vulgar—to ask God's mercy on the unbelief of Israel is a fact I find extremely significant.

1. This very passage was, in fact, altered and the offensive reference deleted by John XXIII in March, 1959, but I have retained the quotation since my remarks are directed to a broader and certainly unresolved issue.

I find this fact particularly significant in view of the equally pertinent fact that Israel provides as well a liturgy of prayer on behalf of the unbelieving nations of the world. And these presumably include the nations in Christendom. Two prayers in the liturgy of Judaism come to mind immediately—not prayers attendant upon specific events or crises of faith, but general, daily, and repeated prayers.

The former of these prayers affirms that God never rejects his elect, that he will deliver his people from the midst of nations, that through Israel's unity the nations will come to worship and glorify him alone; while the second prayer, the better-known *Alenu,* reaffirms the conviction of God's unity and prays that the world will be united under his dominion, that idolatry will wither and pass away, that "the inhabitants of the world may know and acknowledge that unto Thee every knee must bow, and every tongue swear; before Thee, O Lord our God, they shall kneel and fall prostrate; and all of them shall willingly submit to the power of Thy kingdom."

The prayer of Good Friday and the prayers of the synagogue, though directed to the same unity of belief, are obviously incompatible. And their incompatibility points toward profound differences between the Christian and the Jewish approaches to history and world problems. Where the Christian, with prophetic casuistry, reads Jewish hopes as having already been fulfilled, the Jew affirms that, pretensions to the contrary, idolatry persists, the nations are in unbelief, and only at the end of days will God's elect be fulfilled and history united under the dominion of heaven.

Where Christianity assumes fulfillment, Judaism denies it. Where Christianity affirms the completion of history (or at least the accomplishment of that instrument whereby history, in God's time, may be completed) Judaism insists upon the open, unqualified, and unredeemed character of history. In sum, where Christianity asks that Israel remove its veil, Israel insists that it is only delusion which imagines that the veil is removed or removable until a true Messiah appears to redeem the time.

These theological differences, fundamental and irreducible, have been obscured in our day. At first glance it would appear that such obscurity is preferable to the bitter and rancorous relations between Judaism and Christianity which prevailed in previous centuries. We must, however, draw certain distinctions before we succumb to the good will which dominates the present moment.

Good will may be profound or superficial—it may arise from the endless resources of human love or it may be the hypocritical posture of human beings who don't care. It is essential to maintain, against the superficiality of contemporary Judeo-Christian fraternity and brotherhood, the fact that Judaism and Christianity divide profoundly. This division is not repaired by the impermanent cement of sociology or the religious ignorance of contemporary man.

Judaism asserts that history is not redeemed. Christianity maintains that it is. This is a fundamental and irreducible disagreement, which divides Judaism and Christianity to the end of time. But this difference is not without consequences for the conduct of world affairs. If the world is unredeemed, there is no normative principle against which to judge world order other than one which takes into account, fully and deeply, the unredeemed character of that order.

The obvious fact that history *does* exist—in spite of the insistence of Christian radicals that its conditions be transcended—is, for the Jew, empirical evidence of a high order that history is not yet marked with the transforming power of the divine. For him, the only principle which can be used to judge history is one which asserts that history is still open—that its time has not come, that however closed from the vantage point of the Creation, it is open from the perspective of its end, consummation, and transfiguration. Where Christianity (in what I take to be its authentic forms) has made the possibility of a new salvation redundant, Judaism must keep it open, because history bears the seed of the true Messiah.

Where Christianity seems to be pessimistic about history, such pessimism is to my mind a betrayal of its own self-definition: there can be no real pessimism if there is a Church, a saving act, a divine intervention that has articulated the basis of reuniting fallen man to his source in God. Christianity should be optimistic.

Judaism, on the other hand, which seems imperturbably optimistic (such optimism is a consequence of the incredibly shallow "me-tooism" which characterizes Judaism on the American scene), should be fundamentally pessimistic. Its pessimism arises from the fact that it has two tasks: to call out to the world's smugness and satisfaction, to unsettle history, to probe its idolatries, its arrogance, its sureness, and at the same time to guard against false hope, caution against deceiving apocalypticism, protect its trust from the disillusionment of false messianism.

Judaism has, I would contend, betrayed itself. Such betrayal is, however, neither a new nor compelling phenomenon in Judaism. The destiny of Israel is self-betrayal and repentance—an endless rhythm of stupid backsliding and regeneration.

Judaism has just passed through a century of backsliding. The transparency of the German-Jewish symbiosis ended in tragedy; the American-Jewish symbiosis repeats the conspicuous pattern of historical Jewish backsliding. It is no wonder that the Jew should backslide in the Diaspora—for the Jew tends to live in two spheres: one, in which he is bound by supernatural ties that never yield to history or to nature; the other in which he is natural man, subject to the temptations of man—the passion for acceptance, wealth, comfort—all the comfort and the ease of the human order.

There is unending tension between his natural inclination and his supernatural vocation. The cultural symbiosis that he has forged between Americanism and Judaism is precarious. There is no need to document this. Will Herberg and others have exhibited how tenuous is the adjustment, how narrow the ridge he walks, how yawning the abyss. The natural man dominates; the supernatural vocation is suppressed.

The medieval confrontation of Judaism and Christianity is singularly unbefitting our time. It came to pass under conditions of the most grotesque and contrived caricature. Characteristic of both Catholic and Protestant images of the Jew was the conviction of his living death. The Jew, having died with the advent of Christianity, must be either ghost or devil to survive so persistently. It never crossed the consciousness of Christian theology that the survival and, what is more, the continued development of Judaism had providential significance for the Jew in opposition to Christianity.

The role which Christianity can perform in the face of contemporary Judaism is to revive the tradition of *adversus judaeos*. As I have tried to indicate, there is considerable basis and motivation for the relocation of religious polemics in our day: if Christianity is true it must be urged in the face of Judaism. It cannot, however, be urged as it was in days past. The triumph of Christianity over Judaism in the Middle Ages was a triumph *faute de mieux*. The Jew was the victim to be treated as Christendom chose—one day succored with kindness, the next day thrown to the flames.

Were this possible in our day—and the secular state has not made this completely impossible—it would accomplish as little now as it did then. The classic form of *adversus judaeos* was unhistorical, because it did not recognize the fact that it opposed only a theological abstraction. How many were the works of Christian apologetics written without the vaguest knowledge of Jews or Judaism, fabricated, without historical qualification, out of the ancient and questionable polemics of the Gospels. The Jew was little addressed. As the literature indicates, many such apologetic works were written to comfort some unlettered divine who was suffering at the hands of a more skilled Jewish dialectician.

The new form of *adversus judaeos* must meet the crucial question of the Jew: what is the evidence of the world's redemption? Construe evidence as broadly as one will—whether it be the evidence of history or the evidence of the spirit—the Jew remains outside Christianity in the conviction that the redemption of the world is a chimera, that what it promises, it does not fulfill.

At this moment of history, religion has been singularly unproductive. Every meeting that I have attended of religious people seeking to articulate bases of common action in a thermonuclear age reduced itself to self-congratulatory platitudes. What becomes clear is that the reach of constructive theology falls short of contemporary events.

Protestantism talks of peace either in terms that would frighten the most ardent Machiavellian or else replays the record of World War I pacifism; Roman Catholicism moves in an atmosphere of moral casuistry—beautifully statistical and well-balanced, but utterly remote. Protestantism tends either toward the moral realism of Niebuhr or sentimental pacifism, while Roman Catholicism tends toward an arid rationalism.

The contribution of a revised *adversus judaeos*, or as this is, a *contra christianos*, to the crises of modern history would lie in the relatively unexplored territory of contemporary statecraft and political theory. There is a prevailing tendency to leave problems of political theory to the experts, whether such experts be professional scholars or professional statesmen. The assumption on which we operate, as Henry Kissinger has observed, is that politics is so totally adventitious that its theory can no longer be articulated.

This assumption demands that human beings trust the prudence of politicians. Having no choice, no control, no principles in terms of which to charge politics with obligations, we abdicate. Needless to say, the willingness to repose confidence in experts creates the preconditions of the authoritarian state. It is evident that the moment the people debar their own intelligence and judgment from competency, they have granted the pretensions of the state to omnipotence and wisdom. We need not delude ourselves, the state—whether democratic or totalitarian by law—will always accept the mantle of omniscience and superior competence. At the lowest level it makes life easier for the state to operate without criticism. It is also a dangerous temptation to carry the egregious burden of statesmanship from simple paternalism to tyranny.

The contention of the Jew in the face of contemporary history is to mistrust its solutions and, in considerable measure, to charge Christianity anew with the burden of proof. If the culture of the West is Christian—as Christopher Dawson, Martin D'Arcy, and other distinguished Catholic theologians assert—there is need to show forth the fabric of that Christianity. If history, however, is shot through with the demonic—as Bultmann, Tillich, and Niebuhr would argue—it must be shown in what sense Christianity functions in the world at all.

If, as the Jew says, history is unfulfilled, and creation is yet open before the end, the Jew has an obligation, perhaps more profound even than that of the Christian, to join issue with history, to ready it for the end. The mere fact that the Jew has no investment in the historical order places upon him, more profoundly, the burden of shaping it.

In essence, my own position is that Jewish messianism does not depend upon the reformation of the temporal order, the transformation of man through extraordinary, but fundamentally terrestrial, means. The crude materialism of early Jewish messianism has been and will continually be purged. It is only the community that can hope to affect society and the state, only the community, preoccupied with the *facta bruta,* not the dialectical abstractions of the human situation, that can hope to affect the total order of power. The community—the family, the religious fellowship, the labor union, to take random examples—alone can hope to restructure primary human relations and ultimately affect the exercise of power. The turning of history to Him who transcends it comes only by the effort to rethink the foundations on which history and power are based.

Christianity is characterized by hope. Judaism is characterized by trust. The hope that what is believed has come to pass and will be justified is Christian hope. The trust that what is not yet, but is yet readied, will come to pass is Jewish trust. The joining of a fulfilled hope and an unfulfilled trust, in mutual encounter with the obduracy of man and the unyielding order of history, is still to be tried. At this juncture, no advent of community, no opportunity for fresh discovery, can be turned aside either by the Christian or the Jew.

# Silence in the
## Aftermath

WHEN IN THE second century Trypho, a rich and cultured Jew of Ephesus, entered into conversation with Justin Martyr, the Greek philosopher, neither was unaware that their well-mannered and cultured exchange was of the utmost religious significance. They managed at this early moment in Jewish-Christian history to carry on a theological communication in which Trypho sought to understand what he took to be the bizarre and distorted beliefs of the Christian and Justin sought to persuade and convert the Jew. The dialogue was civil—it proceeded from a respect for human beings. Its civility, however, in no way compromised its more serious purpose: the desire of Justin to supplant untruth with truth and, by the power of example and argument, to convert.

Undoubtedly, since the dialogue is written by Justin, the arguments of Trypho are more muted than they would be were the argument constructed by a Jew, but this fact does not compromise our feeling that the gracious exchange of appreciations and entreaties and prayers with which Trypho and his friends take their leave from Justin and with which Justin departs from Trypho are genuine and well meant. It may be, since Justin had been a philosopher before he became a Christian and Trypho a man of leisure and security before he met with Justin, that their humanity was sufficient to blunt the bitterness of familiar theological polemics.[1]

This is to say that the Jew and Christian meet first as human beings. The Baptist lay preacher who sought to convert Adolf Eichmann admitted that he could find neither appeal nor warmth in the natural flesh and bone of Eichmann, that it was to his immortal soul alone that he felt himself called to witness and to preach. He cared only for the supernatural remnant of God in that creature, believing—correctly, I feel—that though man may dispose of Eichmann's guilt before nature, God must determine his own justice or mercy toward the spirit.

The difference between the meeting of the Baptist and the prince of genocide and the meeting of Jew and Christian emerges from the fact that, though the former may ignore the natural man in his last hours in order to prepare the soul for its creator, the Jew and Christian meet in the fullness of their humanity, bringing to each other, as did Trypho and Justin, a complexity of natural talents and affections, personal griefs and hopes, historical neuroses, postures, and ploys. They meet first in their natural condition. It is their persons according to nature that permit them to begin their conversation in a spirit of inquiry and charity. Not so the Baptist and Eichmann, who began on different premises—their humanity dissolved by the supernatural task, the one preacher, the other hearer, the one converting, the other reportedly disposed to be converted.

It cannot be denied then that Richard L. Rubenstein's essay, "Jews, Christians, and Magic," *Christianity and Crisis,* April 30, 1962, is correct in his appeal for the confrontation of the human "Christian" and the human "Jew." But where Dr. Ruben-

---

1. This is not to say that Justin's theological polemic does not include such familiar allegations as that of Israel as a deicide people, or such like.

stein would end the conversation by a reduction of Christian and Jew to a common humanity—which presumably is no longer either Christian or Jewish—I would begin the conversation.

There is justice in Dr. Rubenstein's plaint. Undoubtedly Christians have been well trained through centuries of theological exposition to look upon the Jew less as natural creature than as supernatural testimony. But the impetus to Christian construction of the Jew, as was noted by Dr. Rubenstein himself, was given by the Hebrew Bible. The Old Testament prepares the categories of reproof for the Christian—for assuredly the Christian must find it both amazing and unbelievable, if he takes his faith seriously, that the Jew, palpably a messianic creature, should wait throughout Scripture for the Advent of the messiah-king and then reject him when he appears to have come. This fact, more than any other, is what shocks St. Paul into the elaboration of his Christology—the fact that the Jew apparently rejects what he has all along awaited.

However one sets about writing the theological history of Judaism and Christianity, one must reckon with the fact that Christians are severely disappointed with the Jews, and Jews are appalled by the simplism and naïveté of Christianity. It matters little whether Christians consider simplism to be a virtue and Jews consider their consternation to be justified. What matters is that their conduct toward each other reflects an inability to comprehend.

However earnest and urgent he may have made its appeal, Dr. Rubenstein's counter, in the light of this condition, is wholly beside the point. Certainly there is truth in his contention that the Christian has historically fallen back upon a mysterious and magical construction of the Jew, that the Jew is employed in unlikely and irrelevant contexts to interpret social disaster and upheaval to its victims. The Jews are surely a Christian myth—a myth, moreover, with violent and dangerous consequence. None of this is to be argued.

It is one thing, however, to say that the mythologizing of the Jew is exceedingly dangerous and that Christians should beware of exaggerating further the consequences of such mythology. It is quite another to ask, as Dr. Rubenstein does, that the Jew be removed from the theological circle, led outside the thicket of argument, and treated with that love and affection which is possible only between persons, never between communities.

The acceptance of each other's humanity, the acknowledgment that we are persons before we are Christians and Jews, is, I am persuaded, a wholly meaningless affirmation. It is true in only the most limited of senses—senses, moreover, that are irrelevant to any situation in which human beings are *in fact* Christians and Jews. Dr. Rubenstein addresses Christians, under Christian auspices and asks that they suspend their Christianity in order to behave more properly as human beings. This is a usable postulation if one is addressing the nonreligious, who may retain their Christianity and Judaism as but vestigial residues. Such Christians and Jews are far more dangerous, for they sustain the social and psychological animus that the myth engenders long after they have forgotten the myth itself and the reasons for its devising. But it is not viable if one believes being Christian or Jewish enables the expression of one's humanity—that Christian and Jewish beliefs are not encumbrances to the human condition but sources of its clarification.

The real way to understanding is not the way of divestment. If Jew and Christian wish to confront one another, they must speak with all they are and they must grant the real possibility to each other that they may be wrong. Both Christian and Jew must understand that each is a reality born of God and history, that they are a hybrid of the natural and the supernatural, human history and *Heilsgeschichte*. Anything less than this leaves the conversation of Jew and Christian empty of precisely Judaism and Christianity.

The dialogue begun in recent decades between Protestantism and Roman Catholicism is founded upon a regenerate sense that both communities are united by a common witness to Jesus Christ and a conviction that some means must be found in which that witness can be articulated in common. Judaism and Christianity have no such high order of common witness. Their communality is founded upon the Hebrew Bible. This is, however, less than a whole loaf for either, since for the Jew what Rabbinic Judaism affirms about Scripture enjoys an apodictic status that the Christian does not acknowledge. Similarly what the Christian affirms, in the light of the Gospel, about the Hebrew Bible is wholly foreign to the Jewish experience.

What, then, is the foundation of Jewish-Christian dialogue? Dr. Rubenstein defines one possible basis: that we are natural men whose supernatural vocation is a contingent and precarious addendum. But there is another: the possibility that each might be imperfect, if not wrong. In the exploration of this latter alternative lies the real way of communciation, for it gives dialogue the guts and courage it ordinarily lacks.

I can see little purpose in Jew and Christian discussing theology unless, first, they wish to express and thus to clarify their closed systems of thought (but this is talking *at*, it is monologue overheard); second, they wish by clarification to comprehend each other, to draw Christian into the Jewish conviction of the unredeemedness of the world and Jew into the Christian conviction of its salvation (this is talking to a hypostasis, for here only abstract Christian and abstract Jew address one another); and third, they wish to transform each other (this is dialogue, for each addresses the other in the fullness of his humanity and in the fullness of grace). The first alternative runs no risks, for it is but academic exposition; the second runs no risks, for it confronts the doctrinal man who can keep the heart distant from the intellect; but the third runs all risks, for here is the conversation between persons, not in their artificial humanity, but in the completeness of their human-divine predicament.

There is no polarity of Synagogue and Church, only the polarity of two communities, the people of Israel and the ecclesia. Both communities are communities of history and of grace, of the natural and the supernatural. Only when the community of the unbroken covenant confronts the community of the new covenant (that knows not, according to the flesh, the holy seed of Abraham) can there be religious dialogue—for both are complete and exclusive ways before God and both are incomplete ways in the order of time and history.

Surely there can be no disagreement that bad theology leads to dangerous politics. Unquestionably there is a simple-minded pietism that will continue to see Jews as the killers of Christ (it is possible, is it not, that Jews did share in the condemnation of Jesus of Nazareth, though they did not slay the Christ) and Christians as murderers of Jews (they did murder Jews after all, though we are right in doubting that they were Christian in doing so). Undoubtedly there will be continued efforts to correct Christian liturgical works that speak debasingly of the Jews and Jewish texts that misrepresent the spirit of Christianity. The pietism that misrepresents and the liturgies that perpetuate falsehood, however, neither enter into dialogue nor seek to understand.

Why, then, do Jews and Christians berate each other with what they both acknowledge: namely, that man does monstrous evil, that the myths which are perpetuated prepare history for new evil, and that as long as Christians vastly outnumber Jews the likelihood is that they will slay many more Jews than Jews will slay Christians? (What angers me—and it is for this reason that I write this—is that somehow Jews do not acknowledge that in their purely natural condition they could quite as easily slay Christians as Christians slay Jews.)

It should not be forgotten that Abraham would have used the knife on Isaac had it not been for the staying hand of God. This homiletic observation should be enough to suggest that our humanity is indeed defective, that we are all able to turn the word of God into the service of the demonic. This is no more a Christian propensity than it is a Jewish incapacity; rather it is that Christians have lived with power for centuries and Jews have not. The guiltlessness of the Jew is, therefore, more likely his inexperience than his inability.

It is my conviction that Jews should no longer confront Christianity with the iniquities of its history. If Christianity has not the courage and the heart to treat itself to judgment, then surely the Jew will not aid its contrition. And if it has the grace of penance, it will do penance or perish. Let Jews look to their own spirit. Indeed, let Jews stop living off their disasters—for disaster sustains us, but with each disaster the pain lessens and our strength is no less sapped.

Both Christians and Jews would do well to speak with one another about what it is that the Word of God bids them to do and hear and less about what they have not done and have not heard. Only in this way, the way wherein the natural and the supernatural are so joined as to be indivisible (in which the Christian is in fact according to Christ, and the Jew is in fact according to the Covenant) does the way of repair and renewal become possible.

The death of six million Jews has been an incomparable tearing of creation. There are some things that weary of speech; they welcome silence. Death brings to Jewish lips a prayer of glorification that speaks not of death, so let these six million dead rest in peace undisturbed by words of reproach that cannot touch them or regenerate the living who killed them. Silence in the aftermath; words only in the anticipation of new disaster.

# The Jew, Secularity,
## and Christian Culture

It is not congenial to men of liberal intellect to contemplate the renaissance of religious culture in our time. The liberal temper, encompassing as it does more than the disposition of politics and power, is informed by attitudes and influences reflective of the transformation of Western manners, morality, and habits of thought which followed the decline of baroque culture in the seventeenth century and the beginning of the age of secular enlightenment, transconfessional internationalism and the rule of autonomous reason in the early eighteenth. The religious intellect abdicated, religious art declined, theology and philosophy evaporated as objective orders of knowledge, and, what is more urgent, the focus of myriad small communities of disciplined believers and wonderers shifted from the contemplation and service of God into the pursuit of present, diffuse and immanent social ends—wealth, position, natural virtue and complaisance, harmless and perverse sensuality, political power, indeed, all of these self-subsisting dominions of authority which continue to govern the man of today.

There are no longer unitary and cohesive cultures, spanning nations and languages, however much there may be vortices and constellations of concern which in time may generate general culture once more (general culture meaning here those cultures that depend upon the consciousness and force of a transcendent perfection toward which men move, from which men learn, and by which men are agitated to achieve nobility and excellence). The goals of powerful cultures—and there are powerful cultures in this world (however much we may regard them as defective and incomplete)—are partialities, extrusions of historical exigencies, constructs of the exterior man projected and advocated as though they were, indeed, the whole man and the entirety of his destiny. So we may regard the Marxist-Leninist vision, so we may regard the aggressive capitalism of the industralized West, so we may regard self-arrogating democracies, whose totalitarian claims are no less totalitarian for being beneficent. But such a judgment upon the familiar ideologies of the present age rests upon an assumption: if man is no longer that creature who wonders about his origins, his destiny, and his death (that is, if man is no longer contemplatively historical as were the Prophets, Jonah, Job, Ben Sira, the rabbinic homilists of Exodus or Lamentations or as were Eusebius, Lactantius, St. Augustine, or Pascal, but is rather the enjoyer of a spurious, disordered, transitory historical life) then it is proper to regard the cultures of the day as presumptive, not real; indeed, as ideologies with the garb of culture; not as culture in any recognizable traditional form, but culture construed as an embellishment and adornment of naked power. Culture is as man elects to create and believe it—and if man is no longer before the thunder and manna of God (a continuous dispensation, I believe), but limited to an anarchic, evanescent presentness unto finality, then there can be no religious culture of significance and perduration.

Christian culture existed once; it exists no longer. Jewish culture existed once; it exists no longer. Buddhist culture existed once, as did Confucian, as did Muslim; they exist no longer. The

gifts of this world have become too vast and attainable to persuade men, by the discipline and deferment of expectation, to
await the gifts of grace for which one works diligently and
quietly and without the publicity of the world's appreciation.
Such cultures did once exist—architects, painters, sculptors,
scholars, and mystics, worked anonymously, known only to their
friends, their patrons, and their community; but unknown to the
world except through the glory of their works and the remembrance of God. They were nourished by tradition, succored by
holy conversation, renewed by retreats, prayers and meditation, inspirited by the knowledge that the pleasure of their works was
incommensurate to its rewards and independent of its posterity;
and strengthened in the now-lost wisdom that time mattered little, for a thousand years were yet and still as yesterday in the
perspective of eternity.

It is insufficient to bemoan the passage of religious culture—
the wearisome complaints of Christians (and most vocative com-
plainers in the West on this count are Christians) who hawk the
death of both the West and Christianity, are very often in the
unhappy predicament of not understanding or caring to understand what has really taken place in the modern world. The complaint is less to move the world forward than to regain the time
past, less to roll back the darkness of cruelty, poverty, dispossession and war than to recall earlier dispensations which were able
to rationalize and beatify them as consequences of Adam's fall,
the human condition, the unredemption of man and history. But,
thanks to many auspices, such a pacific acceptance of the human
condition no longer obtains. From Vico and Condorcet to Camus
and Sartre, the image of sanctified progress and the accommodation to absurdity and inauthenticity have made all the achievements and defects of our humanity ours alone both for good and
for evil.

It could not be hoped that what has preceded will persuade my Christian readers that the present age of secularism—that massive desacralization of existence which we have all encouraged and of which we are all the issue—is the reasonable consequence of our freedom, the diffusion of power, the presence of egregious social and economic deprivation, and the emergence of compensating ideologies. You will be, as I am often, tempted to put aside the modern temper as but a willful and punishable excess against the magnificent past. But we would be wrong. It may best be demonstrated that we would be wrong if I array the multitudes of my own past which illustrate the decline of religious culture and exemplify the qualities which give me, if not the assurance, at least the hope, that it may be reborn one day.

The Jew was, with the Greek, the creator of the West—of Western Christianity and, not a little less, of Islam. We were that isolate, uncontaminate, obstinate, and unyielding people whom God, in a moment of superb and excellent capriciousness elected to be his own—much against our protest and conniving as well as with our agreement and joy. In that ancient world, surrounded by a superfluity of gods and the influences of many cultures and polities, my ancestors fashioned a remarkably comprehensive and embracing culture—a culture which synthesized adversity and opposition, which formed a unity out of contrast, which consolidated worship and literature, poetry and imagination in order that its microcosmic world might authentically reflect the macrocosm of the inhabited world.

The Jew was a historical creature; his culture was formed out of the shards and figurations of history—recalling past and limning future, expostulating against waywardness and desecration, prophesying the issue of bad faith and open trust. Whether or not the scroll of Deuteronomy had been found by the prophetess and recalled to Israel, whether or not Ezra had returned from the Babylonian exile and assembled the people of Israel to hear Torah reproclaimed, what may be noted in the Bible is that the Israelites were concerned that the vision of a consecrated people, who knows and transmits knowledge, be sustained.

The first age of Jewish religious culture—the Biblical culture which is called by non-Jews, the Old Testament—is that hoary testament which establishes the first self-conscious, historical antiquity of all our pasts. The Jews wrote self-conscious history because in that bare land—mythically a land of milk and honey—rock and stubby mount, desert and forest were transformed from nature into the matter of history, nature ceasing in its infinitude to protest against time and submit, as the Psalmist repeatedly stresses, to become the harbinger and witness to historical time. Nature became the metaphor for history; the natural dumb show of the Greek became the exemplification of life lived and "the heavens," indeed, "declare the glory of God."

This first and primordial age of religious culture informed by a unique and pre-emptive divinity is the age of the Bible. It could not be hoped that those Hebrews, few in number and without the talent and nurture for power, would be emboldened in the centuries that preceded the rise of Hellenism, to seek the conversion of the world. The Jews believed in their possession of truth (for how else could one imagine their insane struggle even then to endure), but they had the prudence to know that paganism was less an arrogant pretension, than a folly ("For they have eyes but see not, ears but hear not, noses, but they smell not . . ."—folly and untruth, but not until the days of Antiochus Epiphanes and Rome, arrogance and blasphemy); moreover they had the realism to judge history, not in the light of some imminent end which pressured action and decision, but with the perspective of centuries where all works out slowly, patiently, with the humanly unreasonable deliberateness of a God who will not hurry.

The Jews were concerned that they form themselves in order to endure before the assaults of the world (I regard this sense of history—the deliberate patience of God before the impatience of man—as a crucial factor in the Jewish refusal to accept then or now any penultimate redeemer). The culture which the age of Ezra the Scribe transmitted to the teachers of the first centuries of the Common Era was an unsettled culture, a living culture which every day encountered its opposition in the Roman settlements of Palestine, the Greek communities of Northern Palestine and Syria, the mixed cultures of the Diaspora already settled by hundreds of thousands of Jews. Each day these people, who lived, prayed, studied, taught, pilgrimaged to the Holy Land, and died in their dispersion, were reminded of the contrast between their way and the bizarre ways of paganism. They were, as classic exponents of anti-Judaism argued, the nonconforming, alien, unassimilable ferment of their world—refusing false allegiances, distinguishing the proper claims of state from the higher claims of revealed truth, denying obeisance where such was an untenable arrogation or blasphemy. These ancient Jews set the pattern for what was to become the Christian disclaimer before Rome. And, it should not be thought that, in their refusal to remove the sacred from the profane, they denied the rightful claim of secular authority. Not in the least. They were well instructed to acknowledge the legitimacy of power rightfully employed—to command obedience to order, the established just law, the economic sustenance of the state by right payment of tithes and taxes, indeed, to the support of the law of the land. But they refused the right of any prince to command the capitulation of the mind or the spirit to the ordering discretion of the state, holding as they did that the state could command only to the extent of its competence, that it could not teach what it was not endowed to know.

This ancient world wherein pagan and Jew lived together passed. In its passing the West was inhabited by Christian and Muslim, each commanding a vast suzerainty, each founded upon a revelation that commended the immediacy of submission to saving truth, each in turn anathematizing the other in ignorance of the other's claim, and each finding the Jew—ancient and stubborn dissenter that he was—the test and touchstone of their truth's viability. The Jew amid Islam pitted jurisprudence against jurisprudence, religious polity against religious polity, ancient claim against ancient claim (for Islam the issue of Messiah was not an issue, for the terrestrial redeemer had come in the figure of Muhammed and the recalcitrancy of the Jew was not centered upon his refusal of this prophet's divine person but upon his refusal of the prophet's teaching); with Christian the Jew was recalcitrant against a person—"the one and only" Messiah who has fulfilled, completed, and consummated all for which Israel waited (for the Christian, not Judaism, but the unbelieving Jew was the focus of animus; not the system or the Law, but the irreducible, stubborn person of the Jew was the enemy).

The Jew became the pivot of the West—the recipient and reagent of empowered cultures. The unified culture of the Jew disappeared after many centuries of contained existence. Whatever the kings of the Near East had done to pierce the homogeneity of ancient Israel—taking from its midst ten tribes, cutting off captives and exiles, dispersing its adherents—was nothing compared to what Rome achieved. By the time of Rome, Palestine had begun to enjoy the first fruits of secularity (for secularity is born in societies where a settled order obtains long enough to permit the internal contest of ideologies of economic or political privilege and deprivation to constitute themselves), beginning as it did to rationalize the endurance and transmission of an established order of law and custom. The Jew under Rome was already conscious of possessing a rich and bifurcated tradition—formed and blossomed culture ready to be plucked. The culture which the destruction and gutting of the Holy Land ended was a culture already marked by the extremes of ascetic withdrawal and ecstatic apocalypticism and solid middle-class commercial piety, a conservative and a reform party upholding, one the inheritance of the propertied and privileged (whether landowner or priest) and the other the urban middle class and poor, meticulous piety, and inventive spirituality—and each had its supporters, its classes, its conventicles, its subculture within the larger culture that sustained all. Intrepidly and bitterly as they fought, Jewish nationalists (who envisaged God as bound to a single land) and Jewish universalists (who conceived God as having elected one, but not excluded any) perished before sheer might. Judaism went into the Exile; and it entered Exile, according to Rabbinic tradition, with the sorrow of the Divine Presence who was regarded as mourning with it throughout the duration of the Exile until the advent of the Messiah.

Before Christendom and Islam, Judaism was an enduring vestige. To the Jew, Christianity and Islam were regnant kingdoms of error, whom God, in his majesty and justice, would rebuke. Both judgments were, if anything, premature, for all three—Christendom, Islam, and Judaism—have lived until the present and have come to know that each has suffered, and each has been suborned, and each has failed to sustain its covenant. But surely the role of the Jew in the passing of religious culture has been in all truth secondary and tributary to the larger passing of the religious center. What should be asked of us that we be mighty without numbers, persuasive without privilege, influential without an audience?—for the Jew has been disengaged by the design of power from the lifestream of the West for some eighteen centuries. We did more than could have been asked, for we transmitted ancient wisdom to Europe before it sought it, made available manuscripts, scientific and medical knowledge, philosophic wisdom some centuries before scholasticism had been ripened to diffuse it; we preserved the cultures of the ancient world until that moment when, through the leniency and connivance of Spanish Islam, Christian scholars could be instructed to return it to Oxford, Paris, Provence, and Italy.

In short, until the world that the French enlightenment and English empiricism and Dutch and German humanism crystallized independently of Church, the Jew had been the politically disinterested mediator and trafficker in knowledge—without gain or profit, without reward or benefice. I imagine the Jew fulfilled this role because it was an international role—a role which was transmitted without particularity and ethnic allegiance; it was, if you will, a universal role in a world already stubbornly particularist. It is here that I feel obliged to part from Christopher Dawson's estimation of the universality of Christian culture or T. S. Eliot's refusal to allow the entrance of the Jew into his "Christian Society"—for such Christian cultures are universal to Christians, rather than to all men. The marker for both Dawson (positively) and Eliot (negatively) is the generality of the consensus and the removal of dissensus.

There can be no question but that the Jew is an incubus of dissensus. Were we all wise and full of faith, we should be grateful for the dissensus of the Jews and charitable before the vagaries and byways of its present modalities of dissensus.

The Jew is not to be expected to perform as a general culture nor is it, as Max Weber and other social historians casually categorize, a subculture or a pariah culture. We are not a general culture other than prospectively—not a general culture, in fact, for we have not textured or refined the basic history and inheritance of the primary social, political, and communal institutions of the West. We cannot, except by deft handling of Scripture, claim for ourselves either the tradition of the rule of reason and law, the humane foundations of toleration and enlightenment, the touchstones of humanism and political justice; at the same time we cannot, in our conservative passion, bespeak ourselves the guardians of an intellectual aristocracy, a hieratic politics, a dominion of authority by honor, respect, and wisdom. In fact, we can claim any position to ourselves, because it has been the dialectic spirit of our ancient literature—reflecting as it did then a general and total culture—to be the spokesmen of all views and all doctrines. The capaciousness of the classic Jewish temperament should not be mistaken for eclecticism: that the Rabbinic tradition was free and sacerdotal, liberal and narrow, lenient and harsh, bending to the side of mercy or straining to the limit of justice, was—in all its extremity—the reflection of a culture that embraced all kinds of men, but embraced them in a single embrace, for whatever and however Jews then believed they believed out of a fixity of purpose, to know God the better and to serve him with heart, soul, and passion.

As a culture that formed and united a people into a unique service, it was a whole culture and a religious culture. It recognized no sacred and no profane, regarding the sacred as liable to desecration and the profane open to sanctification. The *saeculum*—that forgotten Latin word paralleled in the Rabbinic tradition by the juridic concept of the "public domain"—was the province of the neutral, neither sacral nor condemned. The *saeculum* was the meeting ground of culture, where the exchange and barter of conviction took place, where the rabbis met and conversed with the people, where the homilies and parables of the faith drew their analogies, where, in short, life was lived. The Temple was the arbiter and channel of divine power, the Houses of Study were the *ancillae* of both the *saeculum* and sacerdotal, where truths were formed out of the contact of humanity with revelation, and the Synagogue (before and after the destruction of the Temple) was the extension of study and the divine-human encounter.

Indeed, everything in Judaism was culture—religious culture in its purest and uncorrupted form, for there was no other purpose to culture than to enrich and deepen the mutuality of man and God.

It is an irony that Christian and Jew should come to share the passing of their religious cultures as a consequence of that cycle of historical events which detached the Church from secular power and first secularized the Jew. I do not, Christian historians to the contrary, regard this as the age of secularization (secular, taken here as an absolute and countervailing norm to religion). Indeed, speaking as a Jew, a recipient of the bounties of liberalism, I regard the compact of the Church and State, ecclesia and civil as a much more profound abuse of the religious center than all the devices of a religiously indifferentist modern state. All that has happened today is that the Church and the churches are finding themselves increasingly irrelevant, and, as such, are ignored other than to the extent to which they can effectively compete with political power by the use of political power. For many centuries religious men have failed to speak through the Spirit, but have used the available instruments of coercion, pressure, and ungloved power to hold together a faltering consensus.

At this moment, perhaps for the first time in more than four centuries, there is the hope that the religious man, removed from the councils of power, obliged to rely only upon the persuasiveness of the spirit and the charisma of example, may once more project an image of a more significant enterprise for human life than the routine and terminal self-indulgences which characterize the present West.

The bondage of the Jew amid Christendom need not be rehearsed. It was a long and unremitting bondage, relieved but little, underscored and emboldened frequently. The culture of the Jews of Spain and Provence, a rich and foliated example of infra-culture, was repressed; the conserving culture of north Europe, that of Rashi and the Tosafists in the eleventh century or of the scholars and pious of Germany before the Crusades disappeared; the great centers of Jewry moved again from West to East, disappearing from England, France, Spain, and Germany, reappearing in Italy and Turkey in the south, and Poland and western Russia in the north. All the time these communities were harassed and beset, without other security than wealth or that which influence could purchase (and it could purchase little when communities were already impoverished and depredated); and then, in the wake of the wars of religion in the seventeenth century, an exhausted and debilitated Europe awoke to the nonsense and folly of its fanaticism. For more than a century it had fed on its own bulk, slaughtered its own, destroyed its substance. It could not have been otherwise than that a massive revulsion against narrowness, ignorance, torpidity, inhumanity, and cruelty should gradually alienate man from the intention of religion, and reform persuade him that religion was a secondary, marginal social instrumentality.

The secularity of the European enlightenment was the issue of that more dangerous union of Caesar and Constantine which had been Renaissance Christendom—Catholic or Protestant. Could the French enlighteners or the German humanists or the English rationalists have done other than to ridicule and undermine all that masked its manipulations of power and credulity, anti-intellectualism and superstition as truth. The anti-Church behaved with no more charity or tolerance than did its opposition; the Counter Reformation had been no more palliative and mitigating than had been the Reformation. In the disabusing of Western man of the false power of Christendom, the Jew gradually made his way out of his sectarian culture. The Jew was no longer disqualified merely because of religion—to be sure, he was still by Western Christian standards rude, vulgar, uneducated, ill-mannered, illiterate—hence the peculiar appeal which such a learned Jew as Moses Mendelssohn (died 1786) exercised upon the imagination of educated Europe, becoming, in fact, the example from which Lessing drew his characterization of the tolerant and humane, Nathan the Wise. The educated Jew was a surprise and a delight, because his education was equal to his Westernization, and his Westernization was no less than the turning of his back upon an insulated ghetto culture. The rites of passage whereby the Jew made his way into the West consisted in his de-Judaization. The Jew is secularized (not secular, please note), because the West, the de-Christianized West, made it a condition of his emancipation.

The Jew, in summation, is justly tired of being berated for secularity. It is as though the honorable membership of liberal organizations, civil liberty conservationists, antifanatics are somehow unilaterally subverting an established, accepted, inherited, and unchallenged cultural unanimity—unanimous, that is, until they began to suggest it wasn't. And since it is commonplace for many Catholics and many Protestants to imagine that any Jew who speaks English and lacks beard and frock coat is an atheist secularist, it is well to be reminded of several summarizing consequences of our historical examination:

1. The Jew, by disposition and history, prefers a society where both principle and freedom are inspirited by the religious center.

Jews would have preferred to have shared directly and intimately in the religious nature of Western culture. They were prohibited from doing so by the theological animus of Christendom. They served Christianity, nevertheless, by being the mediators and transmitters of culture, succeeding in this role only by remaining marginal to the dominant culture and insulated within their own.

2. The price of both Jewish marginality and insulation was staggering—the Jew became a myth, and as myth he was slain and reborn endlessly, losing, however, his own real blood along the way.

3. When the internal tension of Christendom was resolved in favor of the neutralization of Christian temporal power, the consequence was that the civil and social life of the West was separated in fact from its spiritual foundations. This separation made possible the normalization of the dissenter; it made possible the normalization and acceptance of the Jew.

4. The Jew, in joining the West, no longer joined a Christian West, for he did not join a Church wedded to a society. He joined an emancipated West (externally emancipated from unjust secular power and internally emancipated from repressive constrictions of thought and imagination). The Jew joined an already de-Christianizing West, and as part of the bargain he agreed—foolishly—to de-Judaize.

5. The mistake of the Jew was that he imagined that the Christian—being French, English, American, Italian, what have you—would be particularist in nationality, but no longer sensitive toward religious difference, having depassed fanaticism for enlightenment. The Jewish mistake was that the very particularity-universality syndrome which makes the Jew both an ethnic (people) and spiritual (universal) phenomenon while being also the citizen of a nation, invited the Christian—however unreligious—

to revive and transmit his "Christian" anti-Semitism of old in the vestments of secularity—economic, nationalist, social, and racial hatred.

It is our contention that Christian culture waned because Christians no longer desired it—that is to say, quite properly, that many Christians (or at least a sufficient number of Christians) have ceased in the present moment to be the Christians of the past. This is not to judge that the Christianity of present-day Christians is less desirable, in principle, than the Christianity of earlier days. As a matter of fact, quite the contrary is my belief. There is greater reason for Jews to trust a Christianity which is without other power than the power of works and grace than a Christianity which also enjoyed the coercive support of the state. For myself, as a Jew, I do not wish for a Christian statecraft any more than a totalitarian secularism—I despise both, for Christianity is destroyed by temporal power and the creative *saeculum* is no longer neutral and open when it becomes totalitarian.

The Jewish contribution—as ancient, medieval, and modern Jew (not as mere Jew-by-birth, or Jew-by-pressure, or Jew-by-sentimentality, or Jew-by-guilt-or-resentment)—can only be made when the Jew is the free *viator* of dissent. The dissent of this Jewish self (and I speak for myself, however much I will honorably acknowledge that I believe my own position to have its share of grand truth) can only exist usefully for the benefit of all men and to the glory of God if it is offered to a free culture, however Christian, Buddhist, or Muslim it might be in generality. To the Christian, my Jewish dissent would warn against an assumption that the First Coming of The Christ is the same as if he had Come Again—that society is still unredeemed, that men are still idolaters, that war, dishonor, meanness, and vanity still render the relations of men brutal and cruel. To the Buddhist, my Jewish dissent would be that his Stoic self-centeredness, whatever the wisdom it may yield the dissolving self, is arrogantly solipsistic in its disinterest in sharing that wisdom directly, actively, passionately with those who become too patient or passive before history. To the Muslim, my Jewish dissent would be against a tradition that has come to make faith a political cause at a moment in history, when the insolvency of nationalism is all too evident to others.

And to all cultures, large and small, this minority culture of Jews can do little more or little less than to continue to speak over and over again those ancient words, "Not by might, not by power, but by My spirit, saith the Lord of hosts." (Zech. 4:6)

# Theological Enmity and
## Judeo-Christian Humanism:
# A Dialectic of the Supernatural
## and the Natural

*A Personal Note by Way of Preface*

THE PESSIMISM implicit in my views of the Judeo-Christian tradition is not final. Pessimism, though perfectly unexceptionable where directed to the silence of nature and the irrational processes of history, is not permissible if one believes in God, not that such belief relieves one of incredible anxiety that frequently topples into the abyss of despair. It is only that the religious thinker must say, as Jews have millennially said, that certain questions await the time of the Messiah for their resolution, and the time of the Messiah is awaited no less urgently by Christians than by Jews. This expectation of the reconciliation of contradiction, the dissolution of paradox, the clarification, in effect, of our human language, is trust for the Jews and hope for the Christians, confident certainty that God will keep his promise to Israel and renew his gift to the Christian community. But all this is at the End of Days and our life amid history and nature offers us but scant encouragement to contemplate those times to come.

In this between-time, in which creation and redemption seem so distant from us and so apposite, there is only the task of living truth. No doubt the living of truth entails the telling of truth and not simply the repetition of truth to ourselves (*sotto voce* and not overheard), but of telling the truth aloud, to one another, over the chasm which separates us from each other and separates us from that completion in God to which we direct ourselves.

Clearly, then, my own pessimism and the anger in which it is frequently expressed in these pages is not final. Mine is an anger against the easy and a pessimism about easy solutions righteously proposed. This concluding essay is, then, more than a reprise and crystallization of my views, for it attempts to point beyond our situation at this moment.

The present is precarious. I could not have anticipated in 1951 when my rejoinder to Nicholas Berdyaev was published[1] that the intransigence of Jews and Christians would soften as perceptibly as it has, that Jews and Christians would in fact be meeting in theological communication, that Pope John XXIII would have altered offensive petitions in the liturgy of Good Friday,[2] that the Declaration on the Jews of the Second Vatican Council would have been so overwhelmingly endorsed,[3] that Cardinal Bea, himself responsible for the drafting of the Declaration, would have written so notable an interpretive volume as *The Church and*

---

1. *Cross Currents*, Spring, 1951, pp. 91-95; cf. pp. 84-91. This essay, published as a Communication, was occasioned by the publication of Berdyaev's "Christianity and Anti-Semitism," *Cross Currents*, Fall, 1950.
2. Arthur Gilbert, *The Vatican Council and the Jews*, World Publishing Company, Cleveland and New York, 1968, pp. 30-31. Gilbert's work is one of the best and most dispassionate records of the Council's deliberations on the Jews.
3. *Ibid.*, p. 161.

*the Jewish People,*[4] that the World Council of Churches would itself have spoken out so forcefully against anti-Semitism,[5] that commissions, Catholic and Protestant, would have undertaken to examine their instructional and petitionary literature to assess the presence of anti-Semitic aspersions and allegations.[6] It would seem that within nearly twenty years the mood has changed. Where before one could have spoken but hopefully of a Judeo-Christian cooperation, that cooperation is today reality. This is, indeed, so. But it is so only in part and in measure. The very truth of that cooperation serves us as a caution, for the truth that it describes is our truth, human truth, and both partial and frangible for all its humanity.

The Jew endures the pain of history and seeks redress from Christendom. This is the plaint of one history to another—the legitimate natural response of the proud victim to the contrite victor, of the victim with a dossier of irrefutable charges and a victor with a bad conscience. There is the inevitable temptation when passionate espousal confronts passionate espousal that truth is dissolved in the alembic of passion. The danger of such dissolution is that in the interest of reconciliation in the public domain, in the order of power and justice, in the arena of interests, in the cause of human fraternity and respect, that ultimate divisions are blunted and compromised. It is an obligation when a blurring of the natural concern for justice and the supernatural conviction of truth occurs that the distinction must be drawn again and, since the distinction has been blurred, drawn more radically, more intensively, more completely. In part, then, the

4. Augustin Cardinal Bea, *The Church and the Jewish People*, trans. by Philip Loretz, S.J., London, 1966.
5. Arthur Gilbert, p. 3f.
6. *Ibid.*, p. 29f.

bleakness of my view is an enforcement of rhetoric. Alas, language compels us to address the head with an unpleasant sharpness lest the good will of the heart close over and soften its thrust. Not that I believe all hearts are good or all heads so susceptible to the temptation to sentimentality. Rather, beyond rhetoric, there is truth here which must be confessed and in the recognition of what that truth entails there is renewed for us a clear grasp upon the realities of our common situation.

If there is one thing and one thing only (greater than all things which *seem* to unite Jews and Christians) which, in fact, unites us profoundly it is that from the same God, from the same creation, from the same stock of history, two faiths, two traditions, two ways of apprehending the existence and mediacy of God have been vouchsafed. These two ways are in opposition and, given the centrality of that event upon which they diverge—that Israel makes Torah the Way and Christianity makes Jesus Christ the companion of the passage—both traditions are in utter, endless, and irresolvable opposition. The one thing that unites us in the order of faith is theological enmity; the one thing which makes possible the commonalty of enmity, the vision of a society in which men may take their stand within the truth and "battle" against each other without mutual destruction, is that it is for the truth that the struggle is joined. It is dishonest for the truth to be described as though the truth did not matter, as though the need of man for human justice entailed the dissolution of the seeking for ultimate truth. Clearly orthodox Christians will not permit this; nor will orthodox Jews. They take the truth and the enmity whole, but they have little vision of the human uses of enmity; and in so far as they lack the courage or the humanity of their enmity, they preserve aloofness and distance. The others, the theologians of natural conscience and liberal good will, would wish to salve truth with the ointments of human concourse, forgetting that however much they may wish to bury differences and conceal their enmity, they betray their faith.

It is, then, my task to accomplish two objectives here: to display the groundwork and historical background of the theological enmity of Judaism and Christianity, to demonstrate its ultimacy, and, indeed, its own contribution to the truth, and, secondly, to expose the tradition of humanism in a light which enables theological enmity in the domain of supernatural truth to become constructive human labor within the precincts of history.

## Myth and the Judeo-Christian Tradition

It is not at all clear whether the energetic myths are ever fully conscious or submissive to the vicissitudes of history in the same manner in which fundamental human institutions, such as family and societal arrangements, are. Those conscious myths, those whose imagery and grammar is universal, always and at every time, are subject to the modifications which exegesis and historical interpretation may bring to them, but they remain substantially unaltered through time. It is curious that those myths which we find it necessary to demythologize[7] have been sustained and transmitted by active institutional custodians, while other myths, no less primary and decisive, remain relatively untouched by historical exigencies, attracting quite the contrary, not an enterprise of demythologizing, but of remythologizing and reinstatement. Among the former are such as the myths of the creation of the world, the paradisical garden, and the original sin of Adam. These myths, however they may point to the enthronement of an

7. Cf. "The Past and Future of Eschatological Thinking," pp. 3-30. Also Rudolf Bultmann, *History and Eschatology*, University Press, Edinburgh, 1957.

omniscient and powerful deity and describe both his promise to created things as well as the original guilt of his defective creatures, require demythologizing in our time because of the consistent inability of men to acknowledge the correlation of poetic and ontological truth.

Scientific criticism—whether deriving from the natural sciences, psychology, or literature—has succeeded in debunking the primal myths of the Hebrew Bible. It is perhaps more accurate to say that the critique of Biblical myth has been most astringent and effective almost in precise relation to the dogmatic centrality which the myth occupied within the traditions of Synagogue and Church. Where myths were narrative, exposing a dimension of the human psyche rather than enforcing upon it a structure of obedience or repression, the willingness to endure the myth, indeed, to elaborate and extend its truth has been more commonplace. The conflict of Cain and Abel, the building and collapse of the Tower of Babel, for example, endure as vital myths for they describe a predicament of man without defining a resolution or enforcing an obedient submission. It is perhaps the case that the myths of creation and the flood present the traditional fideist with a mythology which he must pit against the empirical sciences in order that absolute Biblical revelation remain inviolate. God, however, does not suffer from literature, but presumably those who cannot read literature or else read literature as though it were the actual Word feel themselves deprived of God. Similarly the myth of paradise and the fall of Adam present the Christian with an apodictic demand, for if the world were not in bondage to sin, its ransoming in Jesus Christ would seem needlessly strenuous.[8] This is not the case with the first fratricide, with the

8. The Christian generalization of the story of Adam and Eve into a cosmic myth, implicating the whole of creation, is quite alien to Jewish tradition. Once I thought, when I myself was engaged in dissolving the distinctions

Tower of Babel, with the vow of Jepthe—in these cases the truth is in the drama and the drama is left lean and unencumbered in the telling that those who come after, hearing it, may tremble and be afraid, without concern that either faith or sanity will be undermined.

The Greek myths, those upon which our interpretation of the psychological archetypes of Western man depends, have not themselves been compromised for they have made their way into our history and our unconscious through the mediation of both a regnant Church and secular culture in warm, but informal, compact. Theology and the arts have reworked the Greek myths, and the Greek myths endure. It has not been necessary to take Oedipus or Elektra as enforcements upon our moral will or paradigms of our salvation. As narrative myths, they evoke but they do not oblige. These myths stand and are constantly remythologized for they do not oppose, but rather interpret, the changing sancta of our civilization. It was not necessary for the French Encyclopedists to debunk the life of the Greek gods or the heroes of antiquity. They could remain untouched for they were already myths. Only to the myths that demanded the assent of faith or

---

between Judaism and Christianity, that the communicable disease of sin could be found in Judaism, but this is not so. At most there is a recognition that evil impulse is found in all men, but even if prior to the good (as some sources suggest), it is controllable by learning and right action. The Jews are Pelagian, but since their Pelagianism is no heresy *in se*, the accusation of Pelagianism often leveled against Jewish tradition is meaningless. The Jew is exempted from the Christian theology of the Fall since early-on he came to regard his collectivity as the repository of evil, and sin the privilege of actions, rather than of intentions and desires. For this reason the Jewish interpretation of the sin and banishment of Adam is both genealogically and substantively connected to the crime of Cain and Abraham's decision at Mount Moriah than it is to the divine apostrophizing of man's essential sinfulness.

the compromise of orderly reason was their scorn directed. But then we are not cured of our human needs—infantile or mature— by the exposition of their folly or their unreason. Indeed it is the case that myth is most strong the more profoundly it gives articulate voice to what is most deep, most unspeakable, and most needful in our natures.

The "myth" of the Judeo-Christian tradition is obviously unlike the myths of antiquity. Not unlike them it suggests a reality, but upon explication it does not evoke it, or, when it does, it is inauthentic and unreal. The reality to which it points—the confluence of both traditions, its symbiosis, its mutuality—is a half-truth and a construct. Unlike the myths of antiquity—whether Greek or Hebrew—modern political and social myths fail to address ultimate structures of being. But this need not be pressed. All that is being asserted is that the "myth" of the Judeo-Christian tradition is a myth of modern times. It is an ideological myth and not one which taps the sources of unconscious necessity.

It is difficult to trace the historical origins of the myth. One suspects, however, that its lineaments emerge, first, in the eighteenth century, as a consequence of the critiques leveled by the philosophes of the Enlightenment against revealed religion, second, as a self-defensive gesture of sectors of nineteenth-century beleaguered Christianity, third, as a contemporary formulation of Jews in pluralist America seeking to define a common cause with Christians against secularism and, fourth, as a device whereby Christians affirm a renewed connection with the Hebrew Bible lest the Church once more be accused of fostering that species of Gnostic disconnection out of which the theological polarities of New Testament anti-Judaism issue.

The critique of religion undertaken by the Enlightenment was profoundly antimythological. Whatever its awareness of the luxury and opulence of ancient myth and its delight in the aesthetic vitality and energy of its vision, it had no doubt that it was against reason, and against common sense. But most particularly it was persuaded that the myths of religion produced fanatic narrowness, political repression, and social discord. In the view of the Enlightenment, sectarian religion was the enemy and Christianity was the primary example of sectarianism. It could not be helped that in the attack on Christianity Judaism should suffer, for Christianity depended upon Judaism for the internal logic of its history. However much early Christianity might have sought to polarize itself to Judaism, however much the Fathers of the Eastern Church (and to a lesser extent the Latin fathers) sought to set the ministry of Jesus Christ in apposition to the teaching of the Hebrew Bible, expunging the Gospels of their Jewish roots, cutting off the Church from its involvement in the fortunes of the Synagogue, turning Christianity away from the Jews and toward the pagan world, the philosophes recalled Christianity to its dependence upon the Hebrew Bible.[9] The obscurantism of Christianity—however much it may have been enhanced and reticulated by the original doctrine of the myth of Jesus Christ—depended upon the Hebrew tradition. It could not be otherwise, then, but that a "Christo-Jewish tradition" be one of irrationality and fanaticism, a mythology to be opposed by reason.

The Judeo-Christian tradition is initially a construct of the Enlightenment. At this juncture I do not regard it as a myth, for

9. "The Old Testament, which had served countless generations as an authoritative witness, was in decline: the philosophers used it neither as revealed truth nor as authentic history but as an incriminating document. It revealed, if it revealed anything, the vices of the Chosen People and the tainted sources of the Christian religion." Peter Gay, *The Enlightenment: An Interpretation*, Knopf, New York, 1966, p. 87.

what the Enlightenment set out to destroy was, in fact, accurately perceived. Given its presuppositions, religious fanaticism—growing upon the soil of exclusivities, narrow sectarianism, doctrines of the elect and the damned—contributed to repression, nationalism, and war. It could not but be the case whether the assault be leveled by that Jewish precursor of the Enlightenment, Spinoza, in his *Tractatus,* or later by Voltaire, Diderot, D'Alembert, that the Hebrew Biblical writ was a unit which, despite eccentric theological divisions and disagreements, produced in Christianity a religion to be opposed. The Christian religion depended for its essential theological groundwork upon the religious vision of the Jews and, for that reason, the Christo-Jewish legacy was both affirmed and opposed.

The nineteenth-century revolution in Biblical studies begun by the German school of scientific higher criticism inaugurated the second phase of the history of the myth of the Judeo-Christian tradition. In response, it would seem, to the position of the Enlightenment, it became the concern of Protestant Biblical scholars to disentangle Christianity from its Jewish roots, to split off the Christian experience from that of Judaism and at the same time to naturalize the humanity of Jesus. It became commonplace in this movement of thought to demonstrate that what appeared to the lights of Reformation theology to be most generous, humane, charitable in classic Judaism was really a contribution from outside, whereas indigenous Biblical Judaism was violent, self-righteous, obsessionally paranoid. The Hebrew Biblical tradition was acknowledged, but its nobility and excellence had been taken over by the Church, and what was left over to post-Biblical, Rabbinic Judaism (the Judaism of the Jews) was legalistic, ethnocentric, spiritually defective. From this movement of nineteenth-century thought emerges a species of hypostasis which envisages the benighted Jew of the Old Testament, struggling along with a half-truth, in bondage to a hopeless legalism. On the one hand the genius of the Hebrew Bible is commended; on the other hand Christianity is set in superior condescension to the traditions of Judaism which survive, like ruins, the advent of Jesus Christ, the new architect of mankind. The Judeo-Christian tradition is acknowledged, this time, by Christianity, but no less respondent to the critique of the Enlightenment, by a Christianity anxious to demonstrate that what is correctly denigrated by the Enlightenment is, in fact, the teaching of the ancient Jews whose additions and alterations of the pure Hebrew vision corrupted the source of Christianity.

The higher criticism of the Hebrew Bible became, as Solomon Schechter called it, "the higher anti-Semitism," designed to meet the critique of the philosophes and their heirs in German idealist philosophy by demeaning the Judaic element in Christianity. Whatever truth there is in the scientific criticism of the Hebrew Bible—and there is considerable truth—the ideological impulse was corrupt. The Judaism which survives the onslaught of Protestant Higher Criticism is buried under a mountain of historicist formulations, while a pure, virtuous Kantian Christianity—freed from Jewish accretion—is defined. Once more, almost in recapitulation of the Gnostic tendencies of the early Church (though turned this time to a different task), a "Christo-Jewish" tradition was defined.

The consequence of the de-Judaizing of Christian theology could not be more evident than in the pitiful inability of the Protestant (and to a slightly lesser—but only slightly—extent, Catholic) churches to oppose German National Socialism. It is precarious to make considerations of ethics irrelevant to concerns of theology, to split off the task of living in the world from the pursuit of grace, to make, as many twentieth-century Protestant theologians have made, questions of ethics irrelevant to faith. Among the leaders of the Confessional Churches, only Dietrich Bonhoeffer in Germany and Karl Barth at its borders inveighed against the capitulation of Church to State. Nineteenth-century theologians had, indeed, succeeded: the ethics of the Hebrew Bible were winnowed by the Gospels and the ethics restored to Christian conscience were ethics for the "between-time," when history awaited the return of Christ. The purge of Christianity of its Jewish elements was disastrous. If that was Judeo-Christian tradition—in the spirit of Wellhausen, Kittel (and even most recently Bultmann's *Primitive Christianity*)—the world could not abide it again.

The renewal of the doctrine of the Judeo-Christian tradition, this time liberated from the *ressentiment* of Protestant defensiveness and Catholic *hauteur*, is a postwar phenomenon. Christianity has a bad conscience and Jews seem justifiably content to pique it. Unfortunately the penance which some Christians seem willing to perform and which some Jews seem anxious to exact, whatever its personal value, does not legitimate the creation of a "Judeo-Christian tradition." Clearly it is not denied that both religions share compatible truths. There is a common sacred history; the ethical values to which appeal is made are similar; the eschatological vision overlaps; the normative institutions of both faiths are analogous. Christianity is, as Christians describe it, the younger brother to Judaism and, as Judaism describes it, the daughter religion.[10] To spin, however, from such compatibilities a "tradition," suggests the presence of something more, a *tertium quid* to which both communities appeal and to which both seem more respondent than their historical enmity.

It cannot be doubted that the historical enmity of Judaism and Christianity was real. Before its reality can be abandoned and

10. A. Roy Eckardt, *Elder and Younger Brothers*, Scribner, New York, 1967.

transformed into a new commonalty where humane interests and compatibilities efface historic enmity, the nature of the enmity should be scrutinized. It may, indeed, be the case that what is abandoned now is not truly abandoned, that once more fundamental issues are being glossed and ignored, that the new unity is no less a moral evasion than was the old, forthright brutality. The religious task—whether religion addresses an indifferent world or one aggressively pagan—is to learn how to speak out the truth without feeling the demonic necessity of destroying the world for its sake. The obligation to address the world out of faith, however much a supernatural obligation, can never justify the resort to violence. And yet it would appear that the conviction of liberal theologians, Jewish and Christian, is that the temptation of man to sin is so great and so abiding that the truth itself must be made less dangerous, less blunt, less absolute that the demonic be kept at bay.

## The Theological Enmity of Judaism and Christianity

The covenant of God and Israel is a curious compact—a covenant wherein a people bound itself to acknowledge and serve a demanding God: a covenant wherein an awesomely powerful deity committed himself to protect and succor his people. Not unlike the personal relationships established between other peoples and their gods, the covenant of God and Israel was, nevertheless, remarkable for the austere and complex regimen which it entailed and, over the course of centuries, the incomparable historical self-consciousness which became its most distinguishing feature.

The ancient Hebrews were no less militant and warlike than their neighbors, but their militancy was directed to clearing the land of pagan dissent, of that pagan dissent into which its own adherents were constantly falling. The ambition of other empires was not the ambition of the Hebrews, although to be sure it occasionally fancied itself an imperial power. The Babylonian exile not only put such ambition to rest but occasioned a decisive break with the characteristic theodicy of other peoples—its defeat and humiliation were not ascribed to the weakness of their God nor to his desertion of them, but to his judgment upon their conduct. The megalomaniacal ancient Hebrews made of their God the Lord of history and of their own humiliation the paradigm of retributive justice. God was just in his rebuke, not simply disloyal.

The way of Torah, prescribing the manner in which the People were to serve God and the prophetic instruction by which the People adjusted feeling and intention to the demands of Torah, defined a view of the world radically adverse to the theology of power which characterized other Semitic religions or to the moral perfectionism of the Greeks. The Bible admonishes the individual heart but rarely; it always admonishes the community. The community is neither the surd of power nor the crystallization of individual excellence—it is a whole greater than its constituents, more subject than are its members to the divine judgment. The Hebrews inserted themselves into history as viators and exemplars and, as interpreters and exemplifications, they judged and were judged.

The pathology of the Bible is that it never imagined that it could conquer the world, but it never for an instant doubted that its vision of man and history was the truth. This paradox is both the strength and the enigma of the Jews.

The preceding conspectus of the Biblical view enables us to discriminate the achievement of the Hebrews from the achievements of other Mediterranean or Near Eastern societies. The mythopoesis of the Hebrews was not like that of the Greeks or Babylonians—it did not devolve into the philosophic schools of Athens where the myths of earlier times were taken up and transformed into the analogues of general concepts nor did it remain mired in the acosmic indiscrimination which made time and history an irrelevant medium for the conduct of human and national affairs as in the mythologies of the ancient Near East. The Hebrews discovered history, however much they chose not to write it. They did not produce a Herodotus nor a Thucydides; but, nonetheless, all the books of the Bible suggest that historical time was the conduit through which they passed. Every historical event and occasion was a divine-human meeting, and the freedom to stand ground or turn and flee from the face of God was the essential marker of human response from the times of Abram in Ur to the present condition of dispersion and ingathering.

The Jewish vision of God is in no way marked by Stoic *apathos*—God and the Jews are always engaged; and, as Hebrew poets from Job through the Middle Ages will observe, the flight *from* God is always *to* God, *from* his wrath *to* his mercy. But upon whom is the wrath and the mercy? It is only marginally to the individual. The individual, to be sure, composes a life within Torah that he may celebrate and extend the dominion of God, but characteristically Jewish—in its deepest impulse—is the conviction that before God the single individual may stand and plead only through the merits of the collectivity. Even the age-old intercession that enables the individual to come before God on the strength of the virtues of its Patriarchs, Abraham, Isaac, and Jacob, is a diminution of the atomic self before the historical past. The individual groans for salvation no less because he seeks the redemption of all history before he argues for his own. It is only that the individual Jew is borne on the tides of history, and it is folly to imagine that his merits, achievements, righteousness are ever able to command the attention of a Lord of history.

What is being suggested is that the essential characteristic of the Biblical vision and its consequent elaboration in the Rabbinic tradition is the centrality of history as it both links together creation, revelation, and redemption and as it opposes and countervails it. The whole question of individual worth and individual conscience (or the pedagogy of traditions which would pit against worth and conscience the permanent disability of irremediable sins and primary guilts) falls by the way. The morality of conduct is assessed by the pliancy with which it yields to generalization, its applicability to all men and to the collectivities which they assemble as their means of motion and power. Casuistry, situational ethics, the distinctions and discriminations which occupy the attention of moralists whose concern is the individual, are not usually found in the Hebrew tradition. Even Job, rebelling against his councilors and finally against the theologian, Elihu, is unable to vindicate the claim of the individual—he, too, must finally surrender to the vision of God, the voice out of the wind, who announces once again that "I am" and the sufficiency of that assertion and no more. Job's claims are right—and echoing Abraham, who rebuked God for the disparity between the ways of human and divine justice, he contends that God has treated him cruelly and without justification. To this there is no reply but the disclosure of God's existence and sovereignty. The individual is tried sore but is vindicated, not by exculpation, but alone by the certainty that God lives. God apologizes for nothing. He merely says that he exists.

The Biblical metaphysics is, in my view, dependent upon all the modalities and mutations of historical time. God and the People are the axial bars which intersect historical time and produce in meeting revelation, disclosure, miracle, and mutuality. The People withdraws from each meeting a memorable body of instruction with which to prepare itself for meetings to come. The People makes Law in order to endure the presence of God, and God offers himself to encounter since in the divine pathos the self-visualization of his actuality is, from the view of history, his own potency. The specific character of the Hebrew view of God is that God feels and acts and that the arena of his specific action is the history of the Jews, but in generality the whole of human history.

Jewish messianism is paradigmatically ethnocentric, but really and ultimately is directed to all of history. The messianism begins with the ransoming of the example—the partner in the covenant who is charged "to do and to hear"—and ends with the redemption of all.

It is from the perspective of this view that I regard all attempts to define a Judeo-Christian tradition as essentially barren and meaningless. A historical Judeo-Christian consensus there may be, since the maxims by which both communities instruct their members and inspirit them are common. The grammar and rhetoric of both communities are confluent, the virtues to which they appeal are shared, the moral excellences to which they direct the faithful are compatible; for both there is justice and mercy, wisdom and charity. Of this there is no doubt—and against this who would argue? But at the end point of the consensus, when the good will is exhausted, and the rhetoric has billowed away, there remains an incontestable opposition.

It is usual to formulate the opposition as quite simply the affirmation by Christians and the denial by Jews that Jesus of Nazareth is the Christ. But this is a simplification—a simplification with horrendous consequence. If this were an accurate account of the enmity of Christianity and Judaism, history would have read its outcome rather differently. The assumption of the formulation is that one society of believers accepted, while another denied, the fulfillment of its expectation. The facts, however, are different. What exegesis has made of the record of history and the manner in which exegesis has itself composed the record of history obscure certain crucial considerations. There is no question but that the Jews of the first century, exacerbated as was all of the Near East by portents and signs, natural wonders and historical monstrosities, religious ecstasies and enthusiasms, prophecies and adumbrations, expected a redeeming advent. The Jews were not alone in expectation—Greeks and barbarians, Egyptians and Near Eastern imperials, displaced Romans and alienated Hellenists, all sought a way beyond the depredations, wars, famines, holocausts of history. The Jews no less than others. The Talmud records the coming—and disappearance—of many messiahs, some by name, most anonymously. Messiahs were a Jewish statistic.

There appears, however, one whose obscure origins, humble craft, gentle demeanor, peasant knowledgeability, moral insouciance, ecstatic gift, self-conviction, hieratic arrogance, charisma, sanctity, attracts support. Like others, he threatens and undermines; like few, he has self-knowledge and passion; like many, he frightens and disconcerts; like few, he understands power like his name and intuitively grasps that its most efficient employment is to disdain it; he attracts enemies and he rallies friends; he does miraculously and is treated as a miracle; he denies that he is God, but is pleased to be confused with him. And he comes, as did others, as will others, to the attention of power and like a gnat in the retina of power is rubbed out as cruelly as is a gnat, as would not be a grain of gold; for the gnat can be expunged and the retina will be unscarred, but the grain of gold, removed forcibly, can blind the eye. And so Jesus comes to be crucified, condemned by some Jews, and slain by some Romans. But this eye of power is permanently scarred.

It is the inspiration of history and the compliant tolerance of God that the gnat should become in the eyes of men, not ever again the single madman redeeming his acre of life, but the Son of God redeeming the universe. It is that mad to me. And I cannot but love that madness with all the natural warmth with which I might love any extreme and besetting madness that makes some deserted life bearable, but I cannot, for that reason alone, make of such a life the Messiah or endow such a life, more, with divinity. Not to mention the complexity of trinitarian theology, of the formulations of the Council of Nicea, the canonization of Pauline opinion, as a Jew I am stuck with what I believe—and, like Franz Rosenzweig, I am obliged to say that if I am confronted again with the same madness, the same sanctity, the same fervor, the same conviction, and again if the multitudes contend for its divinity, I am obliged to slay.[11]

11. Franz Rosenzweig, *Briefe*, Schocken Verlag, Berlin, 1935, p. 670-71. Cf. also translation in *Judaism Despite Christianity*, edited by Eugen Rosenstock-Huessy, University of Alabama Press, University, Alabama, 1969, pp. 112-13. The passage to which I allude is that in which Rosenzweig in his correspondence with Rosenstock-Huessy writes: "What does the Christian theological idea of Judaism mean for the Christian? If I am to believe E. R.'s [Eugen Rosenstock-Huessy's] letter before last . . .: Nothing! For there he wrote that nowadays König and he are the only people who still take Judaism seriously. The answer is already on the point of my pen— that it was not here a question of theoretical awareness, but whether there was a continual realization of this theological idea by its being taken seriously in actual practice. This practical way in which the theological idea of the stubbornness of the Jews works itself out, is *hatred of the Jews*. You know as well as I do that all its realistic arguments are only fashionable cloaks to hide the single true metaphysical ground: that we will not make common cause with the world-conquering fiction of Christian dogma, because (however much a fact) it is a fiction (and '*fiat veritas, pereat realitas*,' since 'Thou God art truth') and, putting it in a learned way (from Goethe

Is this not the core of theological enmity? Is this not the charge of deicide vindicated? It is the one. It is not the other. Theological enmity? Yes. Deicide? Not at all. There can be no question but that even in the lucubrations of the Vatican Council the reality of theological enmity, become supernatural, endures. If the Christian faith regards the imperial Christ as compromised not simply by the historical defection of the Jews but by the endurance and flowering of the Jews—despite defection—it is compromised. It may well be the mistake of Christendom to have made of its redeemer so specious a participant in history, that lacking the parousia, it can only record each unfulfilled moment of time as the consequence of Jewish unbelief, but that is to pressure its own theology, for the will of the divine father may be more patient and forbearing than the impetuosity of the divine son. The Church languishes more for the offense to the historical pride of sonship than for the incommunicate patience of the father. But that is a psychologism founded upon a theologoumenon.

The Church demands of the world what the Synagogue will deny it, and the Synagogue must deny it that it endure as Synagogue. Can the Church bear the Synagogue? Yes, if it were an institution of God, but not if it is self-baptized. The predicament of the Church is that that Synagogue not only denies it the condition of fulfillment, but in the logic of Christian history the denial of the Jews itself inhibits the return of Christ. The

---

in *Wilhelm Meister*): that we deny the foundation of contemporary culture (and *'fiat regnum Dei, pereat mundus,'* for 'ye shall be to me a kingdom of priests and a holy people'); and putting it in a popular way: that we have crucified Christ, and, believe me, would do it again every time, we alone in the whole world (and *'fiat nomen Dei Unius, pereat homo,'* for 'to whom will you liken me, that I am like?'')." Rosenstock-Huessy wrote in a later communication that Rosenzweig surely would not slay. And, yes, surely not I, the natural man, who is by training and morality pacific, but I could, like the Dostoevskyan character, be the one-time "holy murderer."

Jews are eternal foot-draggers. But this is theological enmity. This is the drama of those Christians who would *make* God keep his promise (believing that he has broken it) and Jews who would *make* God keep his promise (believing that he has not forgotten it). The one says: he has come, but you slew him and he will not return until your penance glorifies him. The other says: he has not come at all and we are mystified by your historicizing an ancient misuse of power into such a myth. And both say, let him come, that the Kingdom of God begin.

In the order of argument, Christian and Jew are locked in theological enmity.[12] The Jews were corruptible men believing an incorruptible truth, viz., that God cared to enter into covenant with an enclave of history that history might be redeemed. Christians were corruptible men believing an incorruptible truth, viz., that for pagans without a covenant, God would exemplify history through the life and death of a single man that all men, who knew not a Lord of history, would become redeemed men. It is not envisaged by such a view that theological enmity would remain eternal enmity, for the view of the one must join to the doctrine of the other that the whole might be compassed. The Church has been obliged to bind itself to time and history

12. What is argued here can be developed in a comparative history of scriptural exegesis, a comparative study of kairotic events—the destruction of Jerusalem then or the re-establishment of Israel now, in the interpretation of the Exile and the Diaspora as seen by the Church Fathers or as read by Jules Isaac in *Jesus et Israel* or *The Teaching of Contempt*. The dynamics of theological enmity—wherein Christians enforce dishonor upon the Jews and the Jews either sardonically permit their humiliation or else interpret Christian unreason towards them as demonstration of Christian untruth—devolve into natural cruelty. The real issues remain, however, as before, that for one the individual has been saved and history is unredeemed, where for the other history is eternalized and the individual disappears into the collective, for guilt as well as for exculpation. There is no other way, in so far as the history of belief is concerned, to interpret the combat of Jews and Christians.

that its unfulfilled obligation to the unbelievers might be maintained.

What is advanced here is no simple restatement of Franz Rosenzweig's teaching of the two covenants, the divine reconciliation of theological enmity, where both covenants implicitly espouse the validity of the other, each fulfilling a role which the other, by its nature, cannot perform. It is not denied that much of the impetus to my view is owed to Rosenzweig, but no less is owed to earlier Jewish teachers—Maimonides and Jehudah Halevi—who regarded Christianity and Islam as mimetic faiths, compromised in their understanding of God, but clearly preferable in morality and discipline to the theological chaos of paganism.

Rosenzweig, seeking as he did to ground a metaphysics which was structurally prior to faith and, in fact, demanded faith as a noetic principle, was obliged to ontologize historical realities. The Jews and the Christians cease in his analysis to be historical and become hypostatic. The Jew is beyond time and history, eternally present with God, and, therefore, always symbolically at the End, living in the condition of redemption. And though such a Jew is redeemed, his redemption is not complete since it is redemption through revelation, and creation remains, as it was before, untransformed. It is the Christian, always on his way from paganism to the Christ, who is bonded to history and, by implication, whose task it is to unite creation with the *eschaton*. The Jew is the image of redemption which the Christian is obliged to pursue. Understandably, therefore, Rosenzweig suggests that the parousia for the Christian may well be the first coming for the Jew, that the reconciliation will take place at the last moment when the Jew's virtual existence becomes actual in eternity and the Christian has been enabled by Christ to offer history back to God.

Rosenzweig's is heady doctrine and not without considerable merit. It provides the Jew at last with a means of explaining to the

Christian, in essentially Christian terms, why it is that the promise of Jesus to the Jews isn't really interesting. The Jews do not need redemption in the same way as Christians for eternal life, as the Sabbath liturgy affirms, is already "planted in our midst." The regimen of the Jews is the drama of eternity and the Law is but a divine-human convention for setting forth the consequence of God's gift in the covenant. But obviously for the Christian such a view, whatever virtues it may enjoy by acknowledgment of the legitimacy of the Christian experience and hope, is meaningless.

Christian and Jew remain opposed. There is the hard core of invincible ignorance chafing at the imputation that the Jew knows, but is stiff-necked and recalcitrant. The Jew cannot understand how the Christian can speak of redemption in Christ when the world of men and events, even that portion of the world which is baptized out of paganism, so constantly, so meticulously falls back into paganism. For such a Jewish unbeliever—even a Jewish unbeliever with Rosenzweigian doctrine—the Christian is not doing his work. And for the Christian, the encapsulation of the Jew, his insistence upon polarizing the religious life to historical relevance—even where he may accept the Rosenzweigian teaching—is a betrayal. To the one the other is falsely advised. And the impasse remains.

The postulation of theological enmity, notwithstanding its seriousness, must avoid two types of misconstruction, both of which are deadly. Theological enmity is not supernatural, nor is it to be naturally enforced.

The view I have taken throughout these essays and most explicitly here in this concluding essay is that the medium of belief is always history. The knowledge of God, however that knowledge be winnowed of contingency, is still knowledge out of the particularity of the believer. The witness of Abraham on Mount

Moriah which gives to me the example of faithful trust can never be repeated by me—were I presented by God with the occasion —in its exactness. Where I stand before God, no one else stands. The meaning of sacred history, in so far as theology raises the kairotic episodes of history into significant moments of divine-human encounter, may illuminate my situation, may indeed inform me that what I take to be wholly devoid of ultimate significance is, in fact, charged and freighted with ultimacy. Despite the propaedeutic function of sacred history, I am, in the hour of deciding, very much alone. As a Christian I would seek the norm of Jesus as the Christ, and as a Jew I would set myself in the midst of my people; but however I struggle to bring those hypostatic realities to bear upon my time and my hour, my decision is alone before God. Since the medium of the present act is historical—on the narrow ridge, as Buber calls it, between all extremities of faith and faithlessness, eternity and time, truth and deceit, directness and manipulation—can I ever imagine that what I know to be the enmity of theological understanding is absolute before God and therefore obligatory upon imperfect men.

Theological enmity is provisory. It is not a myth in the way in which theological consensus is a myth. It is a fact because we can point to the historical defects by which it has been reflected. The fact is that Christians and Jews *have* projected their enmity as supernatural disagreement and have felt justified, therefore, in the order of natural power in enforcing its consequence. The Christian has misread the crucifixion as deicide and in doing so has made of the corruptibility of historical judgment a supernatural act as though its own perspective were God's. It has been "justified," therefore, in imposing upon the historical Jew the punishment of millennia; and even now in the formulation of the Vatican Council's Declaration on the Jews and its explication by Cardinal Bea there is the unwillingness to recognize that the

Gospels, notably that of St. John, are paranoid in their anger toward the natural Jew. The Christian speaks to the Jew as though its view were that of God, whereas all it possesses is the theological intelligence to interpret and understand what it is God requires. It must care that the judgments it makes upon historical time and the actions it convokes to elaborate them are always regarded as fragile, prudential, and, therefore, dangerous.

Reflect upon Cardinal Bea's tense, involuted, and casuistic interpretation of the charge of deicide and the decision to drop the phrase "guilty of deicide" from the final draft of the Vatican Council's Declaration on the Jews. The critical fact apparent to any casual reader of the Cardinal's interpretation is that, try as he would, with good will and charity abundant, he could not disclaim that Jews composed the Sanhedrin and that Jewish leadership in Jerusalem, however little of it was involved, approved and recommended the condemnation of Jesus. He goes on to argue, again with severe correctness, that those Jews—even those—could not be held guilty of deicide unless they knew that the man whom they condemned was, in fact, a man-God, the Son of God. St. Peter's assertion that "You killed the author of life" is correct, but the aspersion of guilt is removed by his conciliatory apostrophe, "And now, brethren, I know that you acted in ignorance as did also your rulers."[13] At most, the few Jews involved in the prosecution of Jesus can be accused of having complicity with murder, of having authorized the shedding of innocent blood. To them alone might be the judgment of God. But of the people of Palestine, or even to the Jews of the Diaspora, or the Jews of millennial generations thereafter, there cannot be any condemnation of deicide. Despite Cardinal Bea's temporizing, he remains unwilling to forego the conviction that deicide, even if not

13. Augustin Cardinal Bea, p. 69; Acts 3:15, 17.

formally proposed and argued in the Gospels, is, nevertheless, essential to seal the rejection of Israel by Christian history. Had Jesus lived out his life to the end, dying quietly in his sleep, and even thereafter on the third day been resurrected and borne to the right hand of the Father, the grim pathos so characteristic of Christian sensibility would not have existed. The teaching, but perhaps not the man, would have endured. The Passion, however, is the direct object of Christian witness, not the Resurrection. The Resurrection transforms the Passion, makes it right, exhibits its implicit meaning, but it is to the agony of the Passion that the Christian turns in his own anguish. He does not forbear out of faith in the Resurrection, but plunges into the chaos of historical passions, repeatedly, in order to revenge upon history what history did to his God. The natural discharge of stored and preserved anger against the cruelty of the historical is to return judgment for judgment, the lives of millions for one exemplary life.

I can see no way out of this dilemma. The psychological underpinning of the Passion is rage—that life should be so barren, empty, poor, deprived as it is for many men, many faithful, and that those who are accused, those descendants of descendants, though they knew not, though they cared not, should even now, being availed of the teaching, still persist in unbelief. The issue is not whether the accusation of deicide can or cannot be imputed to the Gospels, that the Church does or does not support that accusation, or that it saw fit, as Bea says, for reasons of "pastoral prudence"[14] to omit all reference to the accusation from the Declaration. It is that, however the Church decide in its theological clarity to pronounce, Churchmen are no less children of *ressentiment* than ordinary faithful. They, too, are deprived of justification by the fact that Jews *remain* recalcitrant; when they con-

14. Cardinal Bea, p. 71, n. 1.

demned Jesus the first time it might be said for them that they did not know that he was man-God, but surely after centuries of teaching (and more than teaching) should they not know now? And they do not. They are as recalcitrant as ever, more so, since to the Jewish believer God has signaled some contrary intent by providing history with the occasion for re-establishing the community in its ancient Biblical land.

Must we deny, then, that the accusation of deicide is real? It gives no joy to be accused of murder. The burden of history is not relished. But deicide is one more burden among many that a Jew sustains because he is a Jew of the covenant. In *the order of the historical* the Jew must suffer for having interfered with someone else's quest for transcendental release. But natural pain, physical exhaustion, the weariness of community, the countless dead who must be mourned, the agonies to be remembered, these are all the orderly consequences of having eternal life planted in its midst. And I read "our midst" to mean natural-historical life, one's own flesh, family, *socius*, presence in the world. But in the order of the supernatural, the accusation of deicide is meaningless. No God was slain for none had come. Eternal life, but not man-God, was planted in our midst. No man can slay a God and no *slaying* can be a relevant datum in the order of the *supernatural*. It is clear that here, as one example among many that could be adduced, what is at issue is theological enmity, an enmity which derives from the historical mediation and enactment of an encounter of man with God and a disclosure of God to man.

The theological enmity—the direct and head-on collision of two doctrines of man and two visions of divine grace—have produced, however, not only a misconstruction of the supernatural, but an execrable human cruelty. Clearly there can be no justification for genocide, not even "deicide," although as clearly the accusation of "deicide" has been the origin of the genocide of the Jewish people. The devolution of theological enmity into persecution became the perversion of Christian history. It matters not at all whether Christians acknowledge a "racism" which exceeds the legitimate domain of theological enmity, but there is no doubt that where all are convicted and all are tainted, the acceptable apologetic categories of unbelief and arrogant "shutupness" (in Kierkegaard's phrase) before the truth give way to generalizations of the whole people, their demonism, their miscreancy, their unspeakable corruption. From such specializations of ideology it is no wonder that Jewish history should have become a record of martyrdom. It is equally no wonder, despite the demurrals of Pope Paul, that anti-Semitism, even secular anti-Semitism, should trace its origins to the Gospels and the Church Fathers.[15]

There is no need, as I have argued elsewhere in these essays, to rehearse further the crimes of Christianity against the Jewish people. These crimes are facts. The pathos of these crimes—their needlessness and their inutility—stem from the fact that Christianity misunderstood the challenge of theological enmity and imagined that a contest over truth was in fact a contest over life. This, too, need not be argued. It is accepted. What is not accepted, and for this reason the length and strenuousness of my argumentation, is that accord on the crime of genocide does not mean that the enmity is over, does not mean that reconciliation must be presumed, does not entail disengagement from the contest of belief. There is no point to tolerance where all men are right and in agreement. The test of tolerance is where men combat for truth but honor persons.[16]

15. Cf. Jules Isaac, *The Teaching of Contempt*, Holt, Rinehart & Winston, New York, 1964. Also A. Roy Eckardt.
16. I cannot, in conscience, oppose missionary activity to the Jews, and I endorse missionary witness to Christians. It is an activity I find ultimately unrewarding, for the activity is designed more to enable the missioner to

It is for this reason that the Judeo-Christian tradition is called a modern myth. It is a myth founded on revulsion—the disgust of Jews and the disgrace of Christians. It is the care that both show in their human regard for the other as person that is the appeal of consensual tradition. But as I have argued, the consensus is founded upon the unexceptionable. The acrimony is not even touched by the consensus, the issues are not joined, the hard questions remain unanswered. The only authentic Judeo-Christian tradition is that God bears both communities down to the end of time unreconciled. The Judeo-Christian tradition is that from a common source there should have issued such profound and shattering disagreement. Either that disagreement is explored or, like a knot of bile, it is stored in anger to be vomited in cruelty. Any attempt to smooth over the cracks and fissures of history which divide both communities is not only a disservice to the truth, but is an encouragement to fratricide. We must learn how to live with our enmity, indeed, to make it useful, an agency of natural reconciliation that we may confront each other, not as victims and persecutors, but as men who dispute in the cause of truth.

## Human Fraternity: The Liturgy of Theological Enmity

It is not enough to assert the reality of theological enmity nor to condemn human cruelty which issues from it. To invigorate

---

witness to himself than to bring the unbeliever to believe. Needless to say, where the special psychology of the aggressor is self-vindication, the temptation to misrepresent, to connive and insinuate, to deceive and to trick is often too great. But if to missionize is to bear witness, not to one's self but to the truth and it is in the discourse of truth that the missionary confronts the missionized, it is justified.

the combat over truth is in itself no guarantee that men will not impose their absolutes by tyranny. But there is a process of learning and there is as well the willingness to do human work and leave divine work to God.

The hope which may be brought to the conflict over truth arises less from certainty that human beings are able to control the passions which accompany reflection and belief than from the conviction that whatever the temptations, Christians and Jews are aware of the demonism of which they are capable. It would be easier if we could disavow the enmity, if Jews could abandon their aristocratic *hauteur* before Jesus as Christ and Christians could acknowledge the legitimacy of Torah. But such accommodations are historical concessions which can balsam the abraded surface, but affect none of the deeper sources of the agitation. There are no resolutions possible in history other than the conversion of the Jews or the relapse of Christians into paganism. Assuming that Christians and Jews continue to believe as they have, we must, then, either reckon with the likelihood of a recrudescence of anti-Semitism (translating into social and political terms the ongoing anger of Christendom) or we must find a way of taking the contest of truth and making it a source of human community.

The humanist tradition of the Renaissance suggests certain possibilities which are relevant. It was a classicist humanism, and the concern for man arose less from an ideology of human equality than from the conviction that a common tradition of learning was available to Western man which civilizes the passions, educates the sensibilities, and transcends the borders of class, church, and nation. Learning was without boundaries, and a community of learning, compassing the literature of Greece and Rome as well as that of Gospels and Church Fathers, supplied a coherence and commonalty to literary and intellectual activity which otherwise, limited either to theological pietism or to the contest with ideological heresy, would become repressive and deadly. The later humanism of the Enlightenment, regarded by both its supporters and its opponents as atheist and paganic, nevertheless focussed its critical and creative power upon the liberation of man from fanaticism, parochialism, superstition, irrationality. Both the Christian humanism of the Renaissance and the Enlightenment spirit of pagan humanism are parts of our historical legacy. The question that must be raised is whether, against the background of an essential theological enmity, it is possible to develop the resources of a Judeo-Christian humanism.

The enmity of Judaism and Christianity is founded upon the divergence of images of salvation. It is an appropriate issue upon which to define historical enmity, for the ultimate meeting of God and man in the fullness of time is salvation. But however the disunion of Jews and Christians is understood, before the End, both are incomplete. They are incomplete in their humanity, however virtual their assurance of redemption as believers. It is irrelevant to the condition of fulfillment in faith that Jews (amidst time and history) are already with God at the End or that Christians are redeemed in Christ, if the travail of history in which the humanity of both are tried continues. Elsewhere I have suggested that, theologically speaking, the Exile is the historical coefficient of being unredeemed.[17] What I intended then, referring to a specific condition of the Jews, is generally relevant here. The alienation of the humanity of the believer from God is witnessed to by the perpetuation of a whole variety of human, historical evils—war, poverty, racism, and that ongoing insensitivity, avarice, viciousness, cruelty which make them possible. The historical coefficient of the unredemption of Jews and Christians—what-

17. *The Natural and the Supernatural Jew*, Pantheon, New York, 1962, p. 6.

ever their redemption by faith and service—is that men continue to suffer from those evils which men can cure. Surely one acknowledges the need of grace that the hardened heart be relieved, that care, solicitude, the compassion possible even to the powerful be released, but the quietism which waits upon grace is not tolerable to the oppressed. The Negro no longer waits upon grace, nor does the Israeli, nor does the Latin American, nor do the Vietnamese. There is a weariness with the councils of quietism and whatever their relevance to the interior life, which may be ordered toward God; the world of suffering men and tormented institutions can no longer suffice with their conservative patience.

Jews and Christians have joined together, during these past decades, not alone as men in their naked humanity but as men bearing psalms and seeing visions to oppose the evils of history and to work toward the conditions of peace. They have joined against racism, they have labored against the war in Vietnam, they have been critical of all tyrannies and imperialisms, they have striven against poverty, dispossession, ignorance, disease. It could not be said that Judaism and Christianity have been wholehearted, that official declarations, official movements, official radicalism has defined their common militancy, but that is never and could only be under extraordinary conditions of leadership and spiritual regeneration. It is unquestionable, however, that now, as never before, Christians and Jews have managed to invest their enmity with a common love of the human person and his condition which brunts the hard intransigence of theological vindictiveness and makes of the quest for salvation—even over the chasm of a historical division—an act of loving men. The natural Jew and the human Christian find a common means of incarnating their vision of the Kingdom of God by joining together as faithful to have faith in the historical man and his predicament.

The Judeo-Christian humanism is first and foremost conviction about the need to work within history to make the way smooth for the Kingdom. It matters not at all how God saves us. It is only that he saves us. Levi Yitzhak of Berditchev, seeing before him the destruction that followed in the aftermath of the Napoleonic wars, could pray that God save the Gentiles, even if he delayed in saving the Jews. He intended that the love of man have precedence over theological promises. God will provide his redemption, but man must first offer his human love. The Judeo-Christian fraternity is in the love and service of man—and this in utmost radicality, in utmost criticism of the principalities and dominions of the world which immobilize fluidity of human address, deprive us of openness, deny us access to one another.

The Jew and the Christian care for men, beyond loyalty to any contingent institution which pretends idolatrously to be eternal—whether such be a civil law, an economic doctrine, a society of privilege, a class, or a nation. The Jew and the Christian must come together, therefore, not only as common workers in causes and movements, but as thinkers who must grow to accommodate different conditions of history, whose obligation to reflect upon change and movement is as great as their obligation to preserve ancient prophecies. The prophets of Jerusalem could afford to be general in their search for justice and mercy since all who heard them knew the injustice and corruption to which they spoke. But our ears resonate to other injustices and more subtle corruptions —the racism, poverty, military-mercantile alliances of the ancient world were differently textured and the crimes of that time were differently regarded than the crimes of our own. The ancient Jews coped with the institution of slavery and xenophobic hostility to the pagan enemy, however coupled such were with calls to tolerance and generosity toward the stranger and alien. But then, unlike now, human care for the poor and the dispossessed was uncommonly pronounced, and charity for the orphan and the widow might serve the welfare agencies of our societies with models for moral fervor. In other words, the morality of the Bible can be our morality, but not as a closed codex transmitted without editorial revision. Morality—however we understand natural law—is always an instrumentality of history and must always be adjudicated to authentic needs.

Judeo-Christian humanism must be, then, more than programmatic, speculative, more than directive, prophetic. We cannot raise up prophets who will announce to us what we must do and hear, but we can as men prepare history for the time of salvation, and, however our common action together or our coming to think together, our joining will be prophetic.

Lastly—and I think this aloud with tentativeness—both Jews and Christians in their human concern for human beings have need of the holy spirit, whether the holy spirit be the teaching voice, the *bat kol* of Rabbinic times, the gift of grace. The bringing into our midst of the holy spirit is a task, not alone of prayer in singleness and within our historical liturgies, but in the formation of a liturgical expression of our humanism. The Jew need not learn to hear the Christian speak of the Christ nor must the Christian learn to hear the Jew speak of the dominion of Torah in the time of the Messiah; but both must come to hear in each other the sounds of truth—that the prayer of the Jew is not alone for Jew, but for all men, that the prayer of the Christian is not only for the faithful in Christ, but for all men. It is the commonalty of human suffering that is the commonalty of Christian and Jew; and there must come, as a miracle of grace, a means of expressing that shared experience. Such a liturgy must be a means of purgation—putting to rest the anger which has been the history of Jews and Christians and a liturgy of hope—making appeal to God for the wisdom and forbearance to join together, beyond the temptations of power and divisiveness to serve creation.

Upon one thing Jews and Christians agree: the magnitude of creation and the grandeur and misery of man. Out of such agreement an authentic community, a viable consensus, a meaningful cooperation can emerge—the Judeo-Christian humanism.